K9 DECOYS AND AGGRESSION

ALSO AVAILABLE FROM
DOG TRAINING PRESS

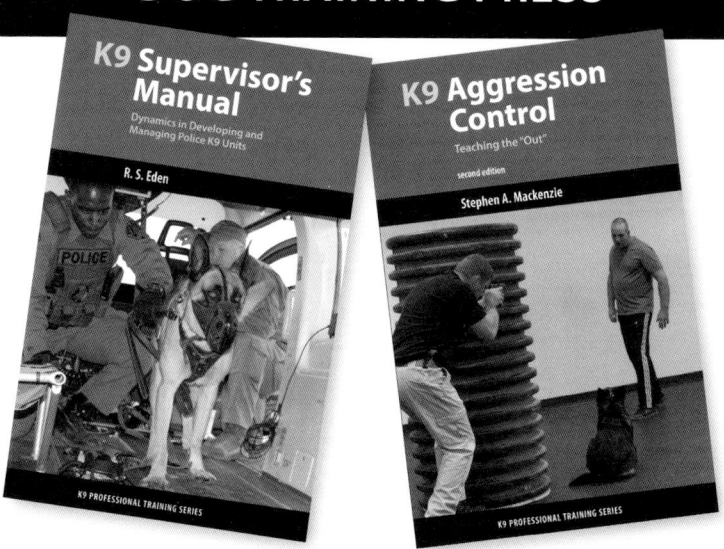

K9 Supervisor's Manual: Dynamics in Developing and Managing Police K9 Units

R. S. EDEN

Understand, oversee, and develop a police-dog program that excels

Learn:
- The five fundamental factors for running a successful unit, and why some K9 units fail
- How to mitigate liability issues
- How to select the right dogs and handlers
- How to handle budgets and deal with police-dog vendors
- Current training trends and how to develop a positive K9 unit culture

2021
Print ISBN: 9781550598889, $44.95
eBook ISBN: 9781550598919, $34.99

K9 Aggression Control: Teaching the "Out"

STEPHEN A. MACKENZIE

A flexible approach to aggression control rooted in obedience training

Learn how to:
- Choose the right dog and training method
- Train dogs that will out reliably in all situations
- Solve common problems in aggression-control training

2017
Print ISBN: 9781550597066, $29.95
eBook ISBN: 9781550597097, $19.99

dogtrainingpress.com

K9 DECOYS AND AGGRESSION

A Manual for Training Police Dogs

SECOND EDITION

Dr. Stephen A. Mackenzie

K9 Professional Training Series

An imprint of
Brush Education Inc.

Copyright © 2015 Stephen A. Mackenzie

25 26 27 6 5 4

Thank you for buying this book and for not copying, scanning, or distributing any part of it without permission. By respecting the spirit as well as the letter of copyright, you support authors and publishers, allowing them to continue to create and distribute the books you value.

Excerpts from this publication may be reproduced under licence from Access Copyright, or with the express written permission of Brush Education Inc., or under licence from a collective management organization in your territory. All rights are otherwise reserved, and no part of this publication may be reproduced, stored in a retrieval system, or transmitted in any form or by any means, electronic, mechanical, photocopying, digital copying, scanning, recording, or otherwise, except as specifically authorized.

Printed in China

Brush Education Inc.
www.brusheducation.ca
contact@brusheducation.ca

Editorial: Meaghan Craven
Cover design: John Luckhurst; cover photo: John Johnston
Interior design: Carol Dragich, Dragich Design
Illustrations: Chao Yu, Vancouver

Library and Archives Canada Cataloguing in Publication
Mackenzie, Stephen A. (Stephen Alexander), 1948– [Decoys and aggression]
K9 decoys and aggression : a manual for training police dogs / Stephen A. Mackenzie. — Second edition.

Revision of: Decoys and aggression : a police K9 training manual / Stephen A. Mackenzie.—Calgary : Detselig Enterprises, ©1996.

Includes bibliographical references and index.
Issued in print and electronic formats.
ISBN 978-1-55059-612-0 (paperback).—ISBN ISBN 978-1-55059-613-7 (pdf).—ISBN 978-1-55059-614-4 (mobi).—ISBN 978-1-55059-615-1 (epub)

1. Police dogs—Training—Handbooks, manuals, etc. 2. Human-animal communication—Handbooks, manuals, etc. I. Title. II. Title: Decoys and aggression

HV8025.M32 2015   636.7'0886   C2015-903969-X
                                          C2015-903970-3

Contents

1. The Role of the Decoy 1
2. Physical Requirements 5
3. Canine Communication 8
4. Human-Canine Communication 33
5. Canine Aggression 43
6. Stimulating and Rewarding Canine Aggression 69
7. Basic Skills 82
8. Common Procedures 101

Notes 153

Index 154

Author Biography 157

Disclaimer

While the contents of this book are based on substantial experience and expertise, working with dogs involves inherent risks, especially in dangerous settings and situations. Anyone using approaches described in this book does so entirely at his or her own risk and both the author and publisher disclaim any liability for any injuries or other damage that may be sustained.

1

The Role of the Decoy

At some point in protection and apprehension training, a person must lure the dog into thinking that he or she is behaving so badly that he or she deserves to be bitten. This person has had many titles over the years. When I first started decoying back in the late 1970s, I was known as an "agitator," since I jumped around a lot and generally got the dogs all excited. Then I found that some people referred to me as a "catcher," since the end result of my efforts was to catch the dog on a protective sleeve. Later, when I started working with sport trainers, people called me a "helper," since my job was to help the dog learn and perfect his skills. Apparently, many of them felt the terms "agitator" and "catcher" were inadequate to describe the scope of the work done. These handles suggest that all the decoy has to do is jump around, annoy the dog, and take a bite in order to do a good job. The scope of the helper's work is, indeed, far beyond that.

At some point in the process of my work someone called me a "decoy," since I was luring the dog into the belief that I was a bad person, a violent criminal, or at least someone who needed biting from time to time. This term has proven to be my favorite in the list, since the decoy not only helps the dog learn but also often uses role deception. When meeting trained dogs for the first time, the decoy performs a valuable kind of dress rehearsal, where the dog thinks the threat is real and the decoy is a stranger. Recently I have heard the term "quarry" used relative to my work, particularly by trainers from the western United States and Canada. It is a good term, but my favorite is still "decoy."

A Valuable Tool

A good decoy is a K9 trainer's most valuable tool. When it comes to aggression work, a good decoy will have a positive influence on the dogs being trained. A good decoy can take a poor dog and make him mediocre, a mediocre dog and make him good, a good dog and make him excellent. A poor decoy can have devastating effects. An excellent dog will become mediocre or worse, as will a good dog. A dog that was mediocre to begin with has no chance at all with a bad decoy; in fact, a bad decoy has the capability to ruin a mediocre dog. In some cases, poor decoys have completely ruined even good dogs. So, the decoy must not only have skill but must also be a disciplined person committed to working cooperatively with the trainer. The decoy's purpose is to provide the trainer with a human being who behaves exactly as the trainer needs at any given time during the dog's development. Consequently, the decoy must be able to act in different manners and change his or her style quickly. In many instances, the actions of the decoy actually control the training and learning process, and there is a tendency for the decoy to begin thinking that he or she is more than just a tool. This is a trap that all good decoys resist, since there can only be one trainer on the field at a time for the best results. Many trainers, having trouble finding good decoys, and having no desire to argue with the big-headed ones they do have, learn to decoy themselves. They realize that when something is really important, they must be able to do it themselves to control the training process.

> A good decoy can take a poor dog and make him mediocre, a mediocre dog and make him good, a good dog and make him excellent. A poor decoy can have devastating effects.

A Communication Expert

The good decoy is an expert in canine communication, understands what the dog is saying at all times, and understands what actions are appropriate to fit the trainer's overall plan for the dog. To do this the decoy begins by studying the paralanguage of the dog until he or she can read dogs well. Then, the decoy must learn how to speak back to the dog, using the same body gestures and behaviors that dogs use to communicate with each other. This, of course, requires the decoy to be in good physical shape and to have timing and coordination—something we will address later.

An Aggression Manipulator

Once he or she is a competent communication expert, the decoy needs to understand the natural forms of aggression in dogs and what behaviors and language will trigger each individual type of aggression. Only then is he or she able to trigger the particular form of aggression the trainer desires at the correct time and avoid triggering aggression when the trainer is trying to do control work.

So, in a nutshell, the following describes the good decoy. He or she:

- reads dogs well
- is in excellent physical shape
- can speak the dog's language
- uses his or her physical skills to trigger or develop different forms of aggression at the proper times
- can avoid stimulating aggression when it is not appropriate

Decoying is a precise skill that requires physical ability and mental discipline. If you desire to prove your courage or are trying to impress people, please stay away from decoying. Eventually you will do something foolish and get hurt, but worse than that, you will hurt a dog, either physically or mentally. If you need to prove yourself, take up something like bungee jumping or sky diving and do us all a favor by leaving dogs alone.

2

Physical Requirements

It is true that almost anyone can put on a sleeve and take a bite, but few people become good decoys. Being a decoy means playing a role in an extremely physical and mental game. It is actually an athletic contest in which the decoy competes with a world-class athlete (the dog). If you are not in peak physical condition, do not expect to excel in this field. I repeatedly see people who are 20 pounds overweight, or breathing heavily due to cigarette use, or just plain weak from being out of shape, trying to decoy. They can let the dog bite them all right, but the dog never gets what she really needs.

When handlers and trainers prepare themselves for the other phases of dog training—such as aggression control or tracking—they first ensure that they have the proper equipment. This is wise. Handlers and trainers would never start an aggression-control lesson without a leash or a tracking session without certain equipment, such as leads, collars, or harnesses, depending on the style of tracking training. They know it is foolish to begin dog work without the correct equipment. And yet they often think they can begin decoy work without a good body. This is a fallacy. The most important equipment for decoy work is a knowledgeable mind inside a sound body, a person who can stand up to anaerobic and aerobic stress, has good upper-body strength, a good sense of timing, balance, quick reactions, and coordination, as well as a strong and healthy back and the ability to absorb pain occasionally. If you would not do control work without the correct equipment, you should not do decoy work without it either.

Which brings us to the difficult part of the story. The above-listed, ideal decoy qualities are essentially God-given gifts encoded in the genetic material of each individual. It is sometimes painful but nonetheless important to realize that some people have these gifts and others do not. Those who have the genetic potential to decoy can also greatly improve their abilities and skills with hard work. However, people who do not have the genetic programming for qualities such as physical coordination and quickness can work hard for their whole lives and never improve enough to become good decoys. Fortunately, everyone has a gift for something. I've always felt that we should not frustrate ourselves trying to do something at which we will never excel.

> **Whatever way you prepare your body for decoying, make sure you are in good shape before you begin working with dogs. You simply have to be in good form to succeed.**

If decoy work is for you, before you begin to train, make sure you have your physician check you out. If you are not in good general health, the extra stress of decoying could be detrimental. Once you have the "go ahead" from your doctor, the next step is to get into shape. This, of course, is a real can of worms since there are many ways in which to do so. Several methods I have seen people employing are dangerous and unnecessary, so be careful about how you approach physical training. There is no quick fix for being out of shape: be prepared to spend some time getting into shape slowly and carefully. If you have pinpointed a method that is approved by your physician, by all means stick with it. If you haven't, you may want to read the *ACSM Fitness Book*.[1] In it, the American College of Sports Medicine describes a method of evaluating your present state of fitness and then suggests a responsible approach to improving it. You could also consult one of the many fitness professionals in your area.

Whatever way you prepare your body for decoying, make sure you are in good shape before you begin working with dogs. You simply have to be in good form to succeed.

One last but important thought. There comes a time in the career of all decoys when they need to stop decoying. Perhaps age, an injury, or failing health is slowing them down. All decoys eventually lose their ability to work effectively. The dogs seem to get faster and the equipment heavier, so decoys begin looking for techniques that require less running. A formerly good decoy who finds him or herself in such a position still has wonderful judgment, however, so he or she may find success in the same field, but in an advisory capacity.

It is difficult for any athlete to recognize when it is time to retire, and decoys are no exception. However, it is important for them to do so. When the time comes, stop decoying. It is better for you, better for the trainer, and better for the dogs.

3

Canine Communication

Once you have established the physical requirements you need to be a decoy, the next task is to study the language of the dog. Decoys must be able to read the dogs they are working with. For example, if a dog's confidence level suddenly changes in the midst of a drill, you must be able to instantly recognize that change. You must also know what the trainer wants you to do if a confidence change should occur. If you always understand what dogs are communicating and react according to a good trainer's instructions, many problems in aggression training can be avoided. Your ability to understand the dog's language and work in harmony with trainers can also help alleviate problems that already exist, either from the dog's basic character or learning from previous training sessions. When decoys are unable to "read" the dog, they are much less valuable and in some cases may even be a hindrance. Any way you look at it, decoys must master the language of the dog to be useful.

Dogs communicate in several ways. Probably the best-known communication method is auditory (with sound). Few people have been around dogs for any length of time without hearing one bark, growl, whine, or howl. All of these noises serve some purpose, although humans do not understand them completely.

Auditory Communication

Research has shown that the pitch and frequency of sound can affect activity levels in puppies regardless of the language trainers use, and handlers have known for a long time that the tone of their voice has a great influence on their dogs' behavior. In the dog world, the higher the pitch of a sound (both emitted and heard by dogs), the more the sound suggests submission, fear, or stress; the lower the tone, the more the sound indicates dominance, confidence, and threat.

The whine is a distance-decreasing signal, indicating that you can come closer; it serves as a plea for assistance. This soft, high-pitched sound is first used by puppies to obtain assistance from the bitch (a technical term for the mother of a dog). It follows, then, that submissive animals whine when they communicate with an upper-ranking animal or authority figure. The function of the whine seems to remain consistent throughout a dog's life: even adult dogs whine when they are seeking help. The yelp is another distance-decreasing signal and is usually a response to physical pain or extreme fear. Dogs interpret these two sounds in the same way, regardless of whether a dog utters them or a human does, so decoys can add to their effectiveness by using yelps and whining noises or other tones of voice when they are trying to convince a dog that he has hurt them and that they are afraid and submissive. Screaming at the dog may be good for realism, but it in no way helps to reward a dog for aggression; yelping and whining do.

The growl is a distance-increasing signal, indicating that you should move away from the dog, and it is usually a form of threat or warning. The growl is often the precursor to aggression and as such can be a sign that the dog is unhappy with something and is considering doing something violent to solve his problem. Although all growls are threats, the voice tone betrays the confidence and stress levels of the dog. The higher the pitch, the more insecure and stressed the dog is, and the lower the pitch, the more confident and serious he is. As a decoy, you can use growls to complement what you are already signaling with your body language. When decoys are using threatening body language, they can increase their effectiveness by uttering a good, low growl. Many high-end dogs—those that are highly motivated, highly reactive, and show high levels of aggression when they react—will show aggression in response to a simple growl, unaccompanied by body language.

The bark is a sign of excitement or high energy and is another distance-increasing signal, indicating that you should move away from the dog. That many stray dogs do not bark suggests that the bark may have something to do with marking or defending territory or personal space. Decoys need to pay attention to the quality of the dog's bark because it indicates the dog's confidence level and therefore the quality of the decoy's work. Again, the voice-tone rule is in effect. The confident dog has a low-pitched bark: low in comparison to what is normal for his breed. As the dog becomes more insecure, submissive, or stressed, the pitch of the bark rises, indicating that he is significantly uncomfortable with what is going on. So, when you are attempting to get a confident reaction from the dog and the dog is barking in a low pitch, all is well. If, on the other hand, you are attempting to get a confident reaction from the dog and the bark is high pitched, something is wrong and you need to change something, such as your distance from the dog or your signals, until the pitch of the bark lowers to normal or below normal. The pitch of the bark can be a real barometer for what you are doing as a decoy.

In addition to the pitch of the bark, you should also pay attention to the rhythm of the barking. Confident dogs often bark in a rhythmical, almost musical, pattern. This smooth rhythm breaks up when they become insecure or stressed. So, when you are trying to get a confident reaction from the dog and the barking is smooth and rhythmical, all is well. If, on the other hand, you want a confident reaction from the dog and the barking is staccato, something about your behavior needs to change so the dog can regain his confidence and his barking becomes smooth and rhythmical again. The voice tone and the rhythm of the bark often go hand in hand, so when you want a confident reaction from the dog and the bark becomes high pitched and staccato at the same time, you know that something is seriously wrong and you need to stop whatever is going on and figure out a better approach.

Sometimes it is the lack of barking that is important. When a dog shows predatory aggression, he wants to close the distance between himself and the prey so he can catch it. Obviously, it would not be useful for him to make a lot of noise and use distance-increasing signals when he wants to get closer to his prey. Barking will work against him in such a situation, so even though he is showing aggression, the dog will become quiet. I have often seen silent dogs with an intense, target-lock on their adversaries. So, if you are trying to stimulate predatory aggression and the dog stops barking and becomes quiet but has intense focus on you, you know you have succeeded. A fully trained dog will often bark even when displaying predatory aggression, but that is a product of training and reward, not a natural reaction.

Other times the lack of barking is a problem. Many dogs have trouble with the Sit and Bark due to an unwillingness to bark at you, the decoy. They are willing to sit in front of you, but they refuse to bark. This is completely understandable if you look at it from the dog's perspective. The bark is a distance-increasing or go-away signal, so to bark is to tell you to go away. The dog does not want you to go away, hence his reluctance to bark. He wants you to stay right where you are and do something stupid so he can bite you and get his reward when his adversary submits. The answer is not to get angry or frustrated with such dogs but instead to teach them that barking will make you take the last step and come close enough to be bitten. Once the dog realizes that sitting and barking will lead to what he wants, life gets a lot easier.

The howl seems to serve as a long-distance marker so that packs can avoid each other's territory in the wild, which lowers the amount of aggression in their lives. It is also a pack-bonding activity and a request for communication at a distance. Any time a dog wants to communicate with someone who is not physically present, he will be tempted to howl. Any time he hears howling (by another dog or in the form of an ambulance siren, for example), he will be tempted to return the howl to report his location to whoever is asking for it.

Olfactory Communication

Dogs also communicate through olfaction (their sense of smell). They often mark their territory by urinating on the boundaries so other dogs will smell their markers and know enough to stay out. There are recorded instances of humans keeping wild wolves out of their camps by urinating around the sites in canine fashion. It is suspected that from the smell of urine, a dog can tell which individual dog marked the spot. Males can certainly tell if the urine is from a female ready to breed. Dogs use the front end of their tongues to force air samples through a small hole between the gums and the upper lip, a process known as "tonguing." This process sends the air sample back above the soft palate to the vomeronasal organ—part of the dog's olfactory apparatus—which gives the dog a better idea of what chemicals are in the air.

The concept of fear scent is a controversial one. Many trainers believe that when human beings are frightened and stressed, they emit a different odor to which dogs react. There are numerous anecdotal stories of dogs with very poor tracking abilities performing almost perfectly on tracks when asked to find criminals who have just committed violent crimes. Some people argue that the human body gives off a completely different odor when the person is afraid, and others feel that it is merely a more concentrated version of the normal body odor, but all agree that dogs can detect the difference and that they react to it in a predatory manner, which in many cases improves performance.

Tactile Communication

Dogs communicate a certain amount through their tactile sense (the sense of touch). The bitch has to lick neonatal puppies (puppies less than three weeks old) to stimulate them to urinate and defecate. She also dries them off and treats their cuts and sores by licking them. As the puppies grow into dogs, licking remains a sign of acceptance, caregiving, or concern. There are similarities between being licked and being petted by a human, which seems to be interpreted by dogs as sign of acceptance, caregiving, and concern. Fast, frantic petting seems to excite dogs, while slow, dull petting seems to have a calming effect.

When the bitch begins to run out of milk and the puppies need solid food, they begin licking and nibbling the bitch's face, which stimulates her to regurgitate partially digested food that they take right out of her mouth. Licking and nibbling the face is one of the first signals puppies give to authority figures. As they grow, this is often used as a sign of respect for a higher-ranking animal.

The bitch often reprimands her puppies with an inhibited bite, which serves to punish them without causing any actual damage. This is frequently seen when the bitch runs out of milk around week seven of the puppies' lives, and she teaches them what has become known as "the one time 'No.'" The puppies have not yet learned that life has rules that must be obeyed, and up until now they have been able to suckle whenever they want. This time, however, the bitch knows that suckling will hurt, and she decides to prevent her puppies from nursing. She usually utters a serious, low-pitched growl to warn the puppies away; they get one, and only one, chance to comply. The problem is that the puppies have never been punished and have no real understanding of what is going on, so they do not comply and continue to approach with intentions of nursing. At this point, the bitch delivers a staggering punishment in the form of an inhibited bite to the puppies' snouts, which make them whine and yelp so loudly that most people fear they may be dying. The puppies learn multiple things from this. First, life has rules that must be obeyed. Second, there are unpleasant consequences when you do not obey them, and third, you only get once chance to comply with directives from dominant animals. These are all things that dogs should understand. Other lessons may occur to you as you reflect on this event. We humans should also learn from this example: punishment is a natural part of the dog world that dogs themselves choose to use. We should notice that the bitch does not use punishment when it is not necessary, but when it is necessary, she does not hesitate to use it and at levels that make it effective. We should also notice that the bitch does not give multiple chances for her puppies to comply, hence the "one time 'No.'" Lastly, we should reflect on the fact that this is the system that puppies are genetically programmed to understand; adult dogs will use the inhibited bite on one another to communicate without causing real damage. If we wish to be well-understood by dogs, we should adopt their patterns. In terms of punishment, therefore, we should only use punishment on our dogs when necessary, but we should not hesitate to use it effectively when it is called for and not give our dogs multiple chances to obey our commands. This is how dogs treat each other when left to their own devices, so we are not unfairly forcing our human values on them if we adopt a similar method. We should always pay attention to how dogs interact with one another so we can learn how best to communicate with them.

> **We should always pay attention to how dogs interact with one another so we can learn how best to communicate with them.**

The style in which a dog bites also carries information. When a dog does not want his prey to escape, he tends to use his whole mouth for biting so as to engage all his teeth and make it difficult for whatever is in there to get back out. This is also the preferred style of biting when a confident dog wishes to keep his adversary under control and dominate it as completely as possible. When a dog is afraid and would prefer the adversary to go away, he bites differently. In this case he does not seek to control but instead to do as much physical damage as quickly as possible so the adversary will be forced to back off or go away completely. To achieve this, the dog sinks his canine teeth into his opponent and thrashes his head around to tear flesh and cause damage. While this is an effective way to defend himself and will hurt the adversary badly, many trainers feel that the slashing style of bite is a sign of insecurity and would rather have a dog that uses what is known as a "full-mouth bite" when engaging a human.

Confident dogs also tend to stay in one place when they bite, getting a good grip on their adversaries and holding on until the fight ends, one way or the other. Insecure dogs, again seeking to do as much damage as possible, tend to bite multiple times, often in different locations so that instead of one or two bites, the adversary suffers several bites and much more damage. In decoy work, sometimes the biting goes up and down the sleeve in what is called a "typewriter bite." (We may have to invent a new name for this soon, since most people are forgetting how a typewriter works.) Occasionally, a confident dog will bite in multiple locations when he is overstimulated and too excited (see the section on the Yerkes-Dodson Law on page 80), but the majority of the time, frantic, multiple bites are a sign of insecurity. For these reasons, many trainers prefer to have a dog that selects the best target area on the adversary and bites there with a full mouth, hanging on without re-biting unless it is absolutely necessary.

Visual Communication

While all forms of communication are important, the greatest amount of information is transmitted visually. Dogs have a precise set of visual signals we have come to call body language. This is the segment of their communication system that is of greatest importance to the decoy. By using personal visual signals in the correct way, different forms of aggression can be triggered at exactly the time you need them for training purposes. Just as important, triggering any aggression can be avoided when it is inappropriate.

READING THE DOG

If you are already experienced at reading dogs, you should probably stick with the method you use now. However, if you are new at the game or do not have an established system for some reason, the following description will help get you started.

Try to look at all dogs in the same sequence so that all of them receive uniform treatment. If you look at the head first one time and the tail first the next, you will eventually miss something important. Also remember to allow for physical causes for the dog's body language. For instance, if there is a noise in front of the dog, and he flicks his ears forward, it probably means he is listening and nothing more. At that point you will have to ignore his ears and read the rest of his body to find out how he feels about what he is hearing. If he slinks around slowly, it may mean he is feeling sick, not that he is insecure. Always eliminate physical causes before you assign emotional meanings to a dog's body language.

It also helps to observe the large indicators first (such as the body axis) and then move to the smaller ones (like the ears and eyes). This can be done in a series of seven steps, beginning with energy level and moving on through body axis, stride, muscle tone, neck, head, and tail.

SEVEN KEY FACTORS IN READING A DOG

1. Energy Level
2. Body Axis
3. Stride
4. Muscle Tone
5. Neck
6. Head
7. Tail

Start by reading the dog's energy level, as is outlined below. Steps two through seven should be read in the order listed, since they are listed in order of importance. In other words, information from each step is more important than information from any of the steps coming lower on the list. For example, if a dog is leaning away from a loud noise but shows confidence in the head and tail, he is showing insecurity, no matter how good the head and tail look. Information from step two is more important than information from steps six and seven. A dog that shows insecurity in all three of the steps just mentioned is in much worse shape than the one whose head and tail look confident, but when signals give conflicting information, give more weight to what you see in the steps higher on the list. This will help you understand ambivalent dogs that send confusing sets of signals.

Those of you who already have an established pattern of reading dogs are probably not going to change your order of observation at this point in your career. My advice is to stay with the pattern you are comfortable with, but add the levels of importance from the seven steps when dogs give you ambivalent signals. If you teach beginner decoys, however, do them a favor and have them learn the seven steps in the order described above. In the long run, they will understand dogs better and read them faster.

ENERGY LEVEL

The energy level is often referred to as the state of arousal. The indicators of high energy are a wagging tail, barking, muscle tremors, faster-than-usual reactions, and a tendency to walk faster or run when not under command. The low-energy dog reacts slowly even when provoked and wants to stop and rest at every opportunity. This tells us nothing about the confidence level of the dog, but high-energy dogs react more quickly and therefore can bite the decoy faster and with less provocation. For your own safety, it is wise to read the dog's energy level before engaging with him.

BODY AXIS

The second thing we look at is the dog's body axis. Ask yourself, "Where is the dog leaning?" Bold, confident dogs stand straight upright or actually lean toward the object of attention. They often stay pointed straight at the object of attention. As they become more insecure or fearful, they begin to lean away from the source of their fear, actually walking backward away from it in extreme cases (see Figures 3.1, 3.2, and 3.3).

Figure 3.1 The body axis of a confident dog.

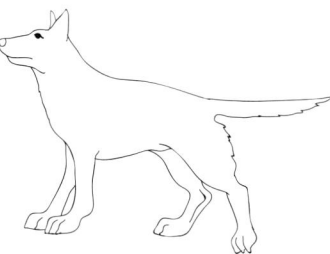

Figure 3.2 The body axis of a less-confident dog.

Figure 3.3 The body axis of an insecure dog.

A fearful dog will also assume a more broadside alignment to the object of attention. In other circumstances, this behavior is part of "T-ing up," where a submissive dog stands still in a sideways alignment to the approach of a dominant dog and allows the upper-ranking animal to inspect him. The dominant dog faces and approaches the lower-ranking dog perpendicularly from the side, usually at the shoulder, forming a letter T. This is a confident, dominant way to approach another animal. The submissive dog is required to remain stationary in the sideways alignment and let the upper-ranking dog inspect him. If he does not do this, he is punished. If both dogs agree that one of them is dominant and the other submissive, no fight will ensue. However, if there is no agreement on which is dominant, the two dogs will jockey for position, each trying to "T-up" on the other, so that both keep moving in circles (see Figures 3.4 and 3.5). This is often a sign that a fight of some sort is brewing.

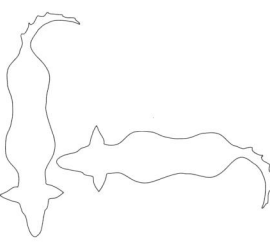

Figure 3.4 T-ing up. The submissive dog stands still for inspection.

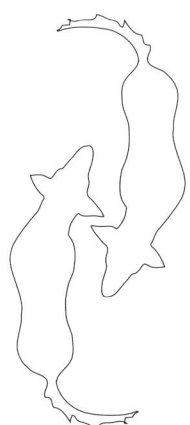

Figure 3.5 T-ing up. Two dogs jockeying for position.

STRIDE

The third item of interest when reading a dog is his stride and leg movements. Dominant dogs approach submissive dogs. Submissive dogs only approach upper-ranking dogs if they are giving numerous submissive signals to accompany such movement. The bold dog stands straight up or moves with long steps that hold the body up away from the ground. As a dog becomes more and more afraid, however, he begins to "slink" by shortening his stride and lowering his body closer to the ground, crawling at some point, until, in extreme cases, he will actually lie down and roll over, lifting his upper hind leg to expose the genital area (see Figures 3.6, 3.7, 3.8, and 3.9).

Figure 3.6 The leg carriage of a confident dog.

Figure 3.7 An insecure dog lowering itself.

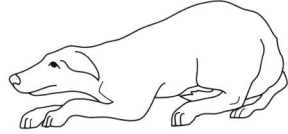

Figure 3.8 A very insecure dog lying down.

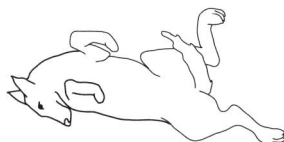

Figure 3.9 An extremely insecure dog rolling over.

Some dogs will even urinate in this situation. A dominant dog will stand over a submissive dog to signal power over him. This movement can be as little as putting his head or paw on top of the other dog's withers (top of the shoulders) as it Ts up, or it can be when the submissive dog lies down and the dominant dog stands with his body over the prostrate subordinate (see Figures 3.10 and 3.11).

On the other end of the spectrum of dog body language, what ecologist and evolutionary biologist Marc Bekoff called the "play bow," is a lowering of the front end of the dog in a bouncing motion of the front legs to signal that whatever follows is not serious, but play (see Figure 3.12). This little bow helps dogs know if they are in a serious fight or a play fight. When it is play, someone bows first.

Figure 3.10 A dominant dog putting his paw on the subordinate's withers.

Figure 3.11 A dominant dog standing over the prostrate subordinate.

Figure 3.12 Bekoff's "play bow."

Figure 3.13 Paw lifting as a sign of partial submission.

Figure 3.14 Paw lifting as a sign of indecision.

There appear to be different meanings—depending on the situation—for when a dog lifts one of his front paws slightly off the ground. After punishment by an upper-ranking dog, this lift is a sign of submission. This is why if, during an obedience workout, your dog raises a paw after a correction, you do not want to get harder with him or you will create overdominance problems. The lifted paw is a very useful signal for trainers. On the other hand, some dogs lift their paw when they are choosing between alternatives (often whether or not they will attack something). In this situation, the lift may be a sign of momentary indecision (see Figures 3.13 and 3.14).

MUSCLE TONE

Muscle tone is the next important indicator you should consider when reading a dog. Walking with stiff leg movements is often practiced by dominant dogs threatening serious aggression while inspecting a lower-ranking animal. On the other hand, fearful dogs will often exhibit muscle tremors, to the point where some appear to be shaking. At first glance, this may seem to be contradictory, but it is not. Dogs that are truly confident in their ability to handle whatever situation they are getting into have loose, relaxed muscle tones. Tight muscle tone usually reflects something less than this complete level of confidence. For instance, if a dog is dominant but not certain of his ability to maintain control, he will have to put on a good show, hence the stiff, strutting walk mentioned above. As his confidence level drops, he will exhibit more and more muscle tension until tremors become visible to the human eye. If you see no tremors, it is useful to put your hand on the dog's chest, between the front legs, to test for them. This is particularly useful for handlers when testing dogs for gun shyness. Slight tremors, invisible to the human eye, can often be detected in this fashion and indicate slight insecurity. Occasionally, a high-energy dog will also have these tremors, but in this case there will be other indicators of high energy present.

NECK

The neck also gives us some information. Confident, dominant dogs approach an adversary with their necks and heads high, often with an arch to the neck. Submissive dogs approach a leader with their necks and heads in a low position. Frightened dogs also carry their necks and heads low. The complication is that when dogs are stalking prey, the neck often carries the head low regardless of confidence level, so the neck must be read in context with the overall situation.

Dogs are said to have their "hackles up" when the hair on the top of their necks sticks up, a condition scientists refer to as piloerection. Like curling the lip, this is an aggressive show designed to make them look bigger and scare another animal away. It is considered a sign of stress, not of complete confidence.

HEAD

The next point of interest is the head. Direct eye contact is often a sign of confidence, even dominance. Predators watch their prey carefully before they attack, and dominant dogs often try to stare down their opponents when trying to T-up with them. Breaking eye contact is usually interpreted as a sign of submission during conflict. Sometimes a submissive dog, standing sideways to the advance of another dog, will actually turn his head away from the dominant animal: the ultimate way of breaking eye contact. An exception to this is when dogs in active conflict turn their heads to the side while still facing their adversaries. At first it appears that they are submitting, but in fact they are daring their opponents to come closer. Further inspection will show they are keeping an eye on their adversaries and are not turning their body axis sideways in submission or displaying any other submissive signals that would make an adversary go away. They are, in effect, luring their adversaries into a trap. When the opponents come close enough, they attack immediately. Many a new decoy has been bitten over the years by misreading this gesture (see Figure 3.15).

A dog's eyes will dilate when he becomes highly aggressive or excited. At this point the tapetum, a reflective layer in the back of the eye, is more exposed than usual, giving the eyes an eerie, crazed appearance. This is often referred to as "showing eye."

Figure 3.15 The trap. Read this situation carefully.

The position of the ears also give us a look inside the dog's mind. The more confident dogs are, the more forward they carry their ears. As they feel more and more insecure, they rotate their ears back until they finally flatten onto the neck. Putting the ears back is also a sign of submission, so take care when interpreting this sign. Many times dogs will submit to things that frighten them, in which case there is little difficulty interpreting the signals properly. However, it is also possible for dogs to feel confident and yet give you leadership rights, in which case the ears may be pulled back in submission while the rest of the body shows confidence.

Another complication relative to ear carriage is that when dogs make the decision to bite, they often prepare for conflict by tucking their ears back into their necks, possibly to prevent damage to them in the coming fight. It is not a sign of fear or submission in this case, but merely a method of damage control. However, while there are always exceptions, confident, dominant dogs generally hold their ears forward, while fearful, submissive dogs pull their ears back (see Figures 3.16, 3.17, 3.18 and 3.19).

Figure 3.16 The ears of a confident dog.

Figure 3.17 The ears of a less-confident dog.

Figure 3.18 The ears of an insecure dog.

Figure 3.19 The ears of a very insecure dog.

Curling the lips back to expose the teeth while growling has been vastly misinterpreted over the years. It is indeed a sign of aggression, but it is not always a sign of complete confidence. It is often an attempt to frighten the other dog and make him move away. Totally confident dogs have no need to make other animals move away; they can handle anything that occurs right up close. Therefore, they stand their ground in confidence and allow you to approach, biting you if need be, but not trying to scare you away. So, curling the lips to show a lot of teeth is considered to be a sign of aggression based on insecurity (see Figures 3.20 and 3.21).

Exposing only a few teeth in the front of the mouth is not considered a major problem and is simply a signal from a confident dog that you should move back, away from him. Dogs that do this are said to have a "short mouth" during aggression workouts. Others show more teeth, retracting the lips farther toward the back of the mouth. This is a sign of greater insecurity, and such dogs are said to have a "long mouth" during aggression work. Some dogs also display a mimic grin that imitates the human smile. This is not common in breeds used for police work, but it does exist and functions as a greeting.

The dog's mouth also indicates to a degree whether the dog is relaxed or tense. When dogs are tense, they often hold their mouths tightly closed and breathe in a controlled manner, whereas relaxed dogs hold their mouths open and breathe in a more spontaneous fashion. Licking the face of another animal is usually a sign of

Figure 3.20 The lips of a confident dog.

Figure 3.21 The lips of a slightly insecure but aggressive dog.

respect or care soliciting. As mentioned previously, puppies learn this behavior when they first do it to stimulate the bitch to regurgitate food for them. Face licking is a manner of approaching a higher-ranking animal when a dog needs something from him or her.

TAIL

The dog's tail gives us a great deal of information. The most noticeable is the excitement level of the dog. When dogs become excited, they begin to wag their tails. Those with docked tails wag their stumps and sometimes their entire rear end. One of the reasons they may be excited is that they are greeting someone they like. Since that is what pet owners see the most, many people think that wagging the tail is a universal sign of friendship and greeting in dogs. This is not true. They will wag their tails any time they are excited. Many will wag their tails while they are biting you during a conflict. After all, that is exciting, too.

The confidence level of dogs is often reflected in how they carry their tail (or the base of a docked tail). Generally, the higher a dog carries his tail the more confident he is. As his confidence level decreases, so does his tail; a truly frightened dog will tuck his tail between his legs. Some dogs will even urinate at this point if they are overstimulated. The dog also uses his tail to indicate respect. Pictures of wolf packs show that only one animal carries his tail above the backbone. This is the dominant male (sometimes the dominant female will do this, too). Everyone else in the pack carries his tail in a lower position. So, carrying the tail high is a sign of confidence, dominance, or both (see Figure 3.22).

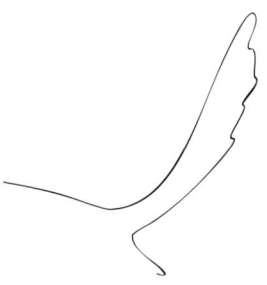

Figure 3.22 The tail of a confident dog.

STANDARD PROFILES

Combining the above body-language pieces can give us some standard profiles of dogs in different emotional states. Figure 3.23 illustrates the appearance of a confident, dominant dog. He stands up straight and tall, faces the object of interest with direct eye contact, holds his ears forward, and has loose muscle tone and a high tail carriage.

Figure 3.24 illustrates a confident dog that is signaling respect to an upper-ranking animal. Note the same body postures on display as in Figure 3.23, except the ears are swept back. Sometimes the dog will look away from the upper-ranking animal to make sure he knows that no eye contact is being made.

Figure 3.23 A composite of a confident dog.

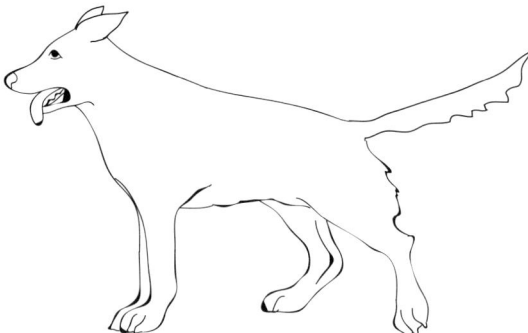

Figure 3.24 A composite of a confident but respectful dog.

Figure 3.25 shows a dog that is fairly confident but not as confident as the dog in Figure 3.24. This dog has shifted his body axis back, his back legs are beginning to lower the body slightly, his neck is slightly lower, and his mouth is shut tightly. This dog is giving mixed signals, so when you read him, be sure to give more importance to the signals that come higher on the list of the seven steps; remember that the ones higher on the list are more important than those that are lower.

Figure 3.26 portrays an example of an insecure dog. This dog's body is leaning back, away from the object of interest. His stride is

Figure 3.25 A composite of an ambivalent dog giving conflicting signals.

Figure 3.26 A composite of an insecure dog.

short, and his muscles are either tight or trembling. Eye contact is broken, the ears are swept back, and the tail is low.

It would take too much time and space to chronicle the other possibilities here, but if you experiment with all possible combinations of the signals, you will be able to complete the list yourself. This exercise is not a waste of time: reading dogs is a lifetime project. A decoy can never claim to be good enough at it.

THREE CATEGORIES OF VISUAL CANINE COMMUNICATION
Most aspects of canine communication can be divided into three major categories that are important to decoys:
- distance increasing (go away)
- distance decreasing (come here)
- arousal signals

Arousal signals show that the dog is excited (i.e., tail wagging). To understand the other two divisions, keep in mind that dogs appear to have set up rules among themselves regarding their use. It seems that only upper-ranking, or dominant, dogs are allowed to use distance-increasing signals when interacting with another dog. Lower-ranking animals are not allowed to control the space around their bodies and are therefore not allowed to tell an upper-ranking dog to get out of their space. If they do this by using distance-increasing signals, they are punished by the dominant dog. Furthermore, they accept the punishment without complaint. It seems that lower-ranking dogs are required to invite upper-ranking dogs into their space and tolerate them there at any time. If the upper-ranking dog traps them in his space, they are required to be extremely respectful and obedient while there, showing respect for the social position of the other dog. You do not have to agree with this approach yourself or think that it is fair; but if you want to understand dogs, you must accept that *they* agree on these rules. This protocol helps dogs maintain order and stability in their world. They set up the rules, not us. So, try to remember that if you are giving distance-increasing signals, you are speaking like an upper-ranking dog, and if you are giving distance-decreasing signals, you are speaking like a lower-ranking animal. The same is true of a dog when he is speaking to you.

DISTANCE-INCREASING SIGNALS
All of the indicators of confidence described earlier are distance-increasing signals and are designed to drive other dogs away or create fear and respect in them. A few, like the lip curl, raised hackles, and stiff leg movements, betray a small amount of insecurity but not much. They indicate a dog that is mostly confident but not completely so.

DISTANCE-INCREASING SIGNALS

1. Facing the opponent
2. Moving or leaning toward the opponent
3. Standing up tall
4. Holding neck and head high
5. Raising hackles
6. Making direct eye contact
7. Holding ears forward
8. Curling lip and/or snarling
9. Holding tail above back
10. Growling
11. Barking

DISTANCE-DECREASING SIGNALS
Conversely, all the signals of insecurity listed earlier are distance-decreasing signals that allow dogs to show respect by inviting the upper-ranking dog into their space.

These signals are of extreme importance to the decoy. By reading these signals carefully, a good decoy knows when to pressure a dog more and when limits are reached. Imitating distance-increasing signals triggers a particular form of aggression in dogs, which I will discuss later. Imitating distance-decreasing signals triggers a completely different form of aggression, and combinations of the two trigger still different types. By sending different signals, you can develop specific parts of a dog's aggressive make-up without overdeveloping others.

DISTANCE-DECREASING SIGNALS

1. Standing sideways or broadside
2. Moving or leaning away from opponent or standing still for inspection
3. Lowering the body
4. Neck and head low
5. Not raising hackles
6. Breaking eye contact
7. Sweeping ears back
8. Not curling the lip or snarling
9. Holding tail below the level of the backbone
10. Whining
11. Not barking

4

Human-Canine Communication

Once you have learned to listen to what the dog is saying, it is time to learn how to speak back. Humans are somewhat limited in their ability to do this, since there are some canine signals that are difficult for us to imitate. For example, we cannot rotate our ears or put them forward and back as well as a dog can, no matter how hard we try. However, there are several canine signals we can imitate, which makes basic communication possible.

Humans can bark, growl, whine, and howl. The quality of these sounds is up for debate, but dogs will respond to our attempts to use these auditory forms of communication. This is why it is important for handlers not to use a whiny tone of voice when giving commands or reprimands. Voice tones are extremely important, since the dog probably doesn't understand the meaning of the words we use in most cases. What she does understand is the noise itself (if repeated consistently) and whether it sounds like a growl (a threat) or a whine (a plea for help or acceptance, usually made by a lower-ranking animal to one of higher rank). Decoys can't mimic the tones of voice dogs can make, but they can actually perform growls and whines to great effect.

Olfactory communication is less valuable in most situations, since it is not socially acceptable for humans to mark their territory exactly the way dogs do. On occasion, humans have succeeded by putting white vinegar into small squirt bottles and marking their territory with that, but something is probably lost in translation.

Tactile communication encompasses many things, so be careful how you touch dogs. Petting and grooming express care and concern about a dog. As mentioned in the previous chapter, humans can communicate excitement through the way they pet their dogs. Rapid movements signal high energy and excitement (and encourage dogs to assume the same condition), while slow, dull petting signals low energy and calm (and encourages dogs to assume the same condition). Pinching a dog's cheeks, ears, or the skin in the flank area (what used to be called "flanking") shows an intent to inflict pain and encourages suspicion and defensive reactions on the part of the dog. Humans don't bite dogs often, but when they do, dogs clearly understand that they are unhappy about something (this is not recommended, since it is a good way to get your face bitten by an aggressive dog). They also understand you are unhappy when you shake them by the neck (when they are small enough), pinch their upper lip into their teeth, or use two fingers to tap them on the nose. They quickly learn that striking causes pain and can easily identify the movements that lead up to pain.

Dogs are the masters of body language, and we need to remember that they are always paying attention to what we are saying, even when we aren't speaking. Handlers and trainers need to make their bodies say the same thing their voices are saying to ensure their messages are being clearly transmitted and received. Decoys need to be able to speak in nothing but body language to achieve the desired results with a minimum amount of stress placed on the dog.

> **Dogs are the masters of body language, and we need to remember that they are always paying attention to what we are saying, even when we aren't speaking.**

The three major categories—arousal signals, distance-increasing signals, and distance-decreasing signals—described in the previous chapter are particularly important for visual signals.

Human Arousal Signals

Arousal signals are expressed by the amount of energy we put into our movements. Wagging the tail is a bit difficult for us, so we have to be content with energy expression and barking-type noises to signal a high state of arousal.

Human Distance-Increasing Signals

Fortunately, we can imitate distance-increasing (go away) signals more effectively than arousal signals. The main problems we have are with raising our hackles (which we can't control voluntarily and don't show well when we can accomplish it), holding our ears in a forward position, and holding our tail above the level of the back. The other signals listed in the previous chapter are possible, which makes our list of major distance-increasing signals a subset of those listed for dogs, with the addition of fast movement of the appendages (hands, arms, feet, and legs) once dogs learn that humans can strike them.

HUMAN DISTANCE-INCREASING SIGNALS

1. Facing the opponent
2. Moving toward the opponent
3. Standing up tall
4. Holding neck and head high
5. Making direct eye contact
6. Curling the lip and/or snarling
7. Growling
8. Barking
9. Making fast movements with appendages

When you face the dog, you imitate the dominant dog approaching the submissive dog. You also imitate a dog preparing to attack another animal. Dogs do not attack well sideways and usually square up on the target before rushing in to attack.

When accompanied by other distance-increasing signals, moving toward the opponent is also interpreted as a go-away signal. Leaning toward the dog is a low-intensity signal, stepping toward her makes it more intense, and actually walking or running toward her is the most intense form of the signal. Increasing the speed of this signal also increases its intensity, so we have an entire spectrum of intensities starting with the slow lean (on the low intensity end), moving all the way up to the fast run (on the most intense end). Again, this signal imitates the dominant dog that moves toward the submissive dog to inspect her. It also imitates the dog actually beginning an attack on another animal; she has to move close enough to touch her opponent or prey before she can inflict any damage.

Standing up tall also imitates the dominant dog in her approach to the submissive dog. The dominant dog usually holds her body as high off the ground as possible, also holding her neck and head high. This is where humans have an advantage. Standing on your "hind legs," you can make yourself look much taller than any dog. So, standing up or crouching down are effective pieces in your body-language arsenal, with the higher postures being the more intense signals for increasing distance. If you hold your neck and head high, you are putting forth a distance-increasing signal for similar reasons. On the opposite side of this spectrum, if you lower your head and neck, you may also break eye contact.

Direct eye contact serves to increase distance for the same reasons as the above-described signals. It is nearly always a component of a dominant dog's approach or actual attack. In particular, before attacking, dogs will usually perform a close, visual inspection of their target, searching for possible weaknesses. A good point to remember with this signal is that humans often wear sunglasses, which prevents the dog from seeing exactly what we are looking at. For clarity in communication, many decoys have developed the habit of turning the entire head when they break eye contact, making it readily apparent when they re-establish it by turning the head back.

Lip curling and snarling are almost as difficult to get humans to do as growling and barking. It just isn't socially acceptable for us to go around making dog faces and noises. These certainly are not the kinds of things most parents encourage in their children, which is perhaps why most of us are reticent to do them. Nonetheless, they are very effective signals when interacting with dogs. It's probably wise not to use them when your parents or in-laws are in town, though.

An important point to remember is that you do not have to actually strike dogs to teach them that fast appendage movements are distance-increasing signals. If fast hand and foot movements are paired with the other go-away signals, they will soon be accepted as part of your collection of distance-increasing signals. Soon after introducing fast appendage movements, the mere raising of a hand will be recognized as a precursor to the rest of the go-away signals and then will become one. No one should use this signal as an excuse to abuse dogs in the name of aggression training.

Human Distance-Decreasing Signals

The distance-decreasing (come-here) signals obviously have the reverse function of the increasing signals. It should be no surprise, then, that in most cases they are simply the opposite of the distance-increasing signals.

HUMAN DISTANCE-DECREASING SIGNALS

1. Turning body sideways
2. Moving away from opponent or standing still for inspection
3. Lowering the body
4. Holding neck and head low
5. Breaking eye contact
6. Not curling lip or snarling
7. Whining
8. Not barking
9. Either slowly moving appendages or not moving them at all

When you turn your body sideways, you imitate the stance of the submissive dog being inspected by the upper-ranking dog. It is also a stance from which one cannot attack an object at a distance efficiently, so it is less of a threat than when you face the dog squarely.

Moving out of the space of an upper-ranking animal shows respect for her position in the pack. So, when you move back away from a dominant dog, you are gesturing submission and inviting the upper-ranking dog to come over to you. There is also a desire on the part of a pack animal—regardless of rank—to maintain contact with the pack. When others move away, a dog is tempted to go in that direction to ensure she does not get left behind. In addition to this, there is a predatory response in dogs that tempts many of them to follow and pursue things that try to move away from them. If moving away from the upper-ranking dog is not possible or desirable, the alternative for the submissive dog is to stand still for inspection and display submissive gestures with the rest of her body.

Lowering the body imitates the submissive or frightened dog that bends her legs to the point of putting her belly on the ground before rolling over. It is a confidence builder for dogs when you let them knock you down when you start a new phase of work or after they have had a bad experience. The effect on the dog of seeing the decoy fall down and stay down in submission so that the dog ends up being taller, or able to actually stand over the defeated enemy, is great. To appear weak to the dog, decoys have been known to work them on their knees, to appear shorter. When the dog is muzzled properly, decoys have also been known to work dogs flat on their backs to let the dogs keep knocking them back down and stand over them until the dog's confidence reaches acceptable levels (at which point they move on to other things).

Holding the neck and head low imitates the submissive dog being inspected and is the opposite of the head carriage of the upper-ranking dog. It also gives the appearance of breaking eye contact. Breaking eye contact is another submissive signal used by any dog showing respect for an upper-ranking dog.

The whine is a plea for assistance, usually made by a lower-ranking dog to a dominant one. It clearly indicates you are submissive.

Dominant and Submissive

Using the above gestures, it is possible for a human to be established as either a dominant or submissive animal, or one that fluctuates between the two. For instance, Figure 4.1 shows a person displaying all distance-increasing signals, advertising himself as a dominant animal. Note he is facing us directly, moving in our direction, standing up as tall as possible with neck and head held

Figure 4.1 A person advertising himself as a dominant animal by using distance-increasing signals.

high, looking directly at us, snarling with lips curled, and (what the picture can't show us) he is growling (when not snarling) and moving his arms in quick, jerky motions. The decoy is telling us quite clearly that he is dominant and that we had better get out of his space, stand submissively for inspection, roll over submissively, or fight. Also note that with the exception of the lip curl, growl, and fast arm movements, this is precisely how the average person approaches a strange dog. Small wonder that most of them get bitten when the dog is dominant or easily frightened.

Figure 4.2, on the other end of the spectrum, shows a person displaying fewer distance-increasing signals than those in Figure 4.1. In fact, this person is putting out ambivalent signals in that some are distance increasing and some are distance decreasing.

Figure 4.2 An ambivalent person displaying both distance-increasing and distance-decreasing signals.

Note that the shoulders are rotated slightly, eye contact has been broken, and there is no lip curl. This person presents much less of a challenge to dominant dogs and is less frightening to the weak of heart. The intensity of the threat could be lowered further if this person were to make whining noises rather than being silent or making deep growling noises. The message? I am a less dominant animal—not necessarily submissive—who does not intend to attack at the moment.

Figure 4.3 shows a person portraying all the distance-decreasing signals. The body is rotated slightly sideways and standing still for inspection (he could also be moving away from us or lying down); and his knees are slightly bent, which lowers

Figure 4.3 A person advertising himself as a submissive animal by using distance-decreasing signals.

the body; his neck and head are held lower than normal, and eye contact has been broken. What the picture can't show is that the arms and legs are still and the decoy is either silent or making whining-type noises. The only way stronger distance-decreasing signals could be given would be if he were to lower his body even more or move away from us. The message this decoy is sending to the dog is that he is a submissive animal inviting the dog into his space. The dog is free to approach as she wishes. This person is no threat to the dog, either physically or socially.

Decoy prospects should practice these signals intensively, until they can switch from increasing to decreasing signals in a split second with no errors. They should be able to display all increasing signals except for one decreasing signal (and vice versa) and then change the contrary signal for another, one at a time, without changing the overall effect of what they are saying to the dog. They should be able to give half-increasing and half-decreasing signals in several combinations without stopping to think about it. This is the language of the decoy. It is what sets the decoy apart from people who merely take bites. Only when you are master of this language can you possibly reach your potential as a decoy. If possible, you should master it before you begin training. If you are already an experienced decoy, mastering it will only improve your skill and worth. Any way you look at it, learning this language forward and backward is time well spent.

5

Canine Aggression

Decoys need to do more than just stimulate aggression in the dogs they are helping to train. They must also stimulate the correct form of aggression at the correct time in the correct amounts. To do this, they must understand what aggression is and of what it is composed. They must also be familiar with the different types of aggression and what body language will trigger each of them.

First of all, let's be clear that when you are decoying dogs you are not activating any "drives," nor are you "putting the dog in drive." There is a certain amount of confusion on this topic due to the misuse of the term "drive." Many new decoys think they are dealing with drives, which accumulate energy that must be released in some manner. This is a natural trap since many trainers use the term "drive" when they really mean "motivation." Since one of the most important jobs of the decoy is to stimulate and maintain the behavior we call aggression, it is worth the time to discuss what behaviors actually are, that they are not drives, and what factors actually do affect them. In this chapter I will discuss this, even as I describe the different forms of aggression and whether or not they are useful in the training of police service dogs.

Aggression is simply a behavior. It is not driven by mysterious forces or drives seemingly understood only by Europeans. Like all other behaviors, it is affected by four major factors and the decoy is part of only one of these factors. Clark Hull's drive-reduction theory attempted to explain behavior and motivation, but it fell into disfavor in the mid-1950s because it was quickly identified as an inadequate and faulty method of describing behaviors. Hull's theory has been basically ignored by serious scientists ever since, giving way to other theories of motivation like Abraham Maslow's hierarchy of needs, the incentive theory of motivation, and others. According to the drive-reduction theory, one drive was supposed to be made up of multiple behaviors so that dealing with one drive dealt with all the component behaviors, making life rather simple. Unfortunately, most behaviors proved to be independent of the others, which resulted in each of them having their own drive, thereby destroying the purpose of speaking about "drives" in the first place. The simplicity of a single drive accounting for multiple behaviors was discredited.

Then there was the problem of attractiveness. For example, if someone who really likes chocolate eats a huge meal to the point where he or she is completely full and satiated, he or she could be said to have completely satisfied the hunger drive and should not wish to eat anymore. If you offer that person a piece of chocolate, however, he or she will eat it, even though the hunger drive is completely satisfied. The reward value of that chocolate explains the behavior when the drive-reduction theory cannot. There are many behaviors that follow this pattern.

If understanding drives was important for training, trainers of all species of animals would focus on them. They don't. If you talk to behavior-problem consultants who work with companion animals, you'll find out that they don't focus on drives. Talk to horse trainers—they don't mention drives. Talk to bird trainers—they don't mention drives. And if you talk to marine-mammal trainers, you'll discover that they don't focus on drives, either. Go to a large academic library and pull out two or three good texts on introductory psychology and turn to the section on drives in each of them. You will probably find that there isn't a section on drives except to mention them as part of the history of psychology. Clearly the concept of drives was faulty in the 1950s, it is still faulty today, and will remain faulty in the future.

So, behaviors are not created and maintained by mysterious forces pushing from behind and forcing the dog to do things. Rather, they are encouraged by genetics and drawn out by what is in front of the dog and the attractiveness of an activity in the pleasure circuits of the brain, specifically the release of the neurotransmitter dopamine in what is known as the mesolimbic reward pathway. Neuroscientists are clear that the effect of the release of dopamine in that part of the brain is what animals find rewarding and so attractive that they will strive to attain it and repeat whatever behavior they think led to it. Apparently, dopamine is the biological basis of reinforcement and motivation.

In the end, the belief in drives excuses sloppy behavior by trainers and decoys, since they feel that the reduction of drive energy carries the day. Modern information suggests that this is not the case and that instead considerations such as good genetics, operant conditioning, positive reinforcement, reward frequency, timing, and value are extremely important. If we stop focusing on drives and pay attention to how we breed and raise our dogs, as well as the details of operant and classical conditioning, we will become better trainers and decoys. Our beliefs affect our actions; so discussion about "drives" is not simply one about semantics.

Behavior

If drives are not controlling behaviors, specifically aggression, then what is? Aggression, like many other behaviors, is affected by four major factors: genetics, chemistry, early experience, and adult learning.

$$B = G + C + EE + AL$$

Where:
B = Behavior
G = Genetics

C = Chemistry (hormones and concentration of neurotransmitters in the brain)

EE = Early experiences (during the sensitive periods of development)

AL = Adult learning (lessons learned from the environment, including trainers and decoys)

Modern breeders will quickly recognize this as an adaptation of the classic equation

$$P = G + E$$

The P in this equation stands for phenotypic, or physical, expression of a trait (in this case the behavior), while G stands for genetics and E for environmental factors. This is the equation that describes the components of quantitative, or polygenic traits, which is what most behaviors of importance to trainers and decoys are. This simply means that most behaviors are influenced by many, even hundreds or thousands of genes instead of just a few and that the environment also affects them.

For our purposes, I have divided the G in this equation into two parts: genetics and chemistry. Most of the enzymes involved with the production and concentration of neurotransmitters in the brain are proteins, and proteins are directly controlled by the genetic makeup of the animal, so genetics and chemistry are probably subdivisions of the same factor in the equation $B = G + C + EE + AL$. It is beneficial to look at them separately, though, because at this point we cannot change the genetic makeup of an animal. Gene splicing is just not a practical or economically feasible approach, yet. Neurotransmitters in the brain, however, are another matter. We can administer drugs and medications to change chemical concentrations, so although imbalances may have been caused by genetics, it is worthwhile considering chemistry separately, since we can do something about that, whereas we are unable to change the genotype of the animal.

I would also split the E for environment into two parts: the effects of the environment early in life during the sensitive periods of development and the effects of the environment in adult life. This is where trainers and decoys fit in. To maximize good behaviors, we must create good genotypes through breeding or biotechnology, raise the puppies well to provide the proper early experiences, and train them well as adults—and we must accomplish all these things in the same dog. If we fail at any one of these steps, we will not maximize the behaviors we are interested in, including aggression. Without a good decoy, the environmental effects will be poor and the quality of aggression will suffer.

> **Aggression, like many other behaviors, is affected by four major factors: genetics, chemistry, early experience, and adult learning.**

GENETICS

Some behaviors are controlled by genetics and require no input from the other three factors. We call these instincts, or instinctive behaviors. The best example is the rooting behavior of newborn mammals that results in the infant connecting to a nipple to suckle. The infant does not need to be raised properly or learn this from others: rooting occurs spontaneously. Many behaviors are not controlled this completely but are strongly influenced by genetics, and others are influenced in a much weaker fashion. The animal is prompted by genetics to try certain behaviors, and the consequences of those behaviors (whether dopamine is released in the reward pathway or not) determine whether or not they are learned and repeated. Most behaviors that are of interest to trainers and decoys, including aggression, show this type of genetic influence. We have known this since the days of W.T. James and his genetic studies in the 1920s and the landmark studies of Scott and Fuller that followed in the 1940s and 1950s.[1] Different heritability estimates in more recent studies show that specific behaviors have differing amounts of genetic influence and that the environment plays a major part in the development of behaviors.[2] This should not be surprising since simple Mendelian sampling will create differences in the genotype of each dog.[3] These differences in the genetic makeup of each dog create different levels of encouragement to attempt different types of behavior, including the different forms of aggression. So, some dogs will be more tempted to engage in predatory aggression, while others will be more tempted to engage in socially challenging forms of aggression due to their genetic differences. Different dogs will seem stronger in different types of aggression, and one of the decoy's jobs is to balance these strengths and weaknesses to shape a dog that is as strong as possible in all the important types of aggression. Genetic influence is also found in the emotional traits fear and confidence, which we need in order to train dogs for apprehension work, as well as the behaviors we need in order to teach to search dogs, such as curiosity and hunting. However, when training dogs we cannot focus on genetics alone, and we cannot ignore genetics to focus on the environment alone. To produce good working dogs, we must properly control both genetics and the environment. The decoy is part of the environment and is thus an essential part of the process.

CHEMISTRY

Concentrations of neurotransmitters in the brain are known to affect aggression levels. Dogs with lower levels of serotonin tend to show more aggression, and the application of serotonergic drugs (drugs that increase the concentration of serotonin) tends to lower aggression levels. Dogs with repetitive behavior problems known as stereotypies tend to have higher levels of dopamine than normal, and lowering this can help them. Medications such as DAP (Dog Appeasing Pheromone) can also help dogs adjust to environments that frighten or make them uncomfortable. Most experts agree that medications should not be used alone as a treatment but rather always in conjunction with good behavior-modification programs. It is difficult to decoy dogs that are concerned about the strange footing they are on or the lack of light in a dark room, or that are feeling anxious because they are separated from their companions, so it is tempting to use medications in such situations. Every rule will have its exceptions, of course, but while medications can be useful to help pet dogs with behavior problems, working-dog trainers and decoys should not rely on them. We do not want to deploy dogs that perform poorly simply because we forget to administer or run out of their daily medications. It is wise, instead, to select and train dogs that have no need for medications in the first place.

> **While medications can be useful to help pet dogs with behavior problems, working-dog trainers and decoys should not rely on them. We do not want to deploy dogs that perform poorly simply because we forget to administer or run out of their daily medications. It is wise, instead, to select and train dogs that have no need for medications in the first place.**

As for hormones, anyone who has worked with bitches in estrus knows that hormone levels affect behavior in dogs. In the male, the androgen testosterone is famous for its effects on aggression and is the basis for castrating male dogs. When deciding whether or not to neuter a male dog to reduce aggression, however, remember that all behaviors, including aggression, have an adult learning component that does not disappear when the chemistry of the body changes. If the dog has been rewarded for being aggressive, the aggression becomes a learned behavior and will be maintained even after the testicles are removed. This is often bad news for companion-dog owners who wait too long to neuter their dogs, but it can be good news for working-dog handlers whose male dogs must be neutered in the middle of their careers due to medical problems. When a good decoy is involved, you often see no difference in aggression levels after castration in the mature dog. You can administer hormones artificially. For instance, the use of progestins has been known to reduce the effects of androgens such as testosterone and consequently aggression in other species. Progestins are synthetically manufactured copies of the female hormone progesterone, which is responsible for maintaining pregnancy and produces the calm, contented behavior of the pregnant bitch. As with the application of medications, hormone therapy should always be done in conjunction with good behavior-modification techniques, and while it may be an advantage for some, it is probably not something trainers and decoys should rely on.

EARLY EXPERIENCE

Once genetics has encouraged the dog to attempt a certain type of behavior, the consequence of that action is important. If the consequence is pleasant, the behavior will be repeated; if it is unpleasant, it will not happen as often and may disappear completely. The first step to thinking something is pleasant is to think that it feels normal, and this is where the early experiences of a dog come into play. All dogs progress through the same developmental stages as they grow up. These stages have become known as sensitive periods, and the one we call the socialization period is probably the most important in terms of the dog's ability to work with a decoy. The best way to understand these periods is to consider what is happening physically in the young dog's brain and nervous system.

Being an altricial species, a dog is born deaf, blind, and mostly helpless, with a nervous system that is not well-organized or even fully connected. The first two weeks of a puppy's life, known as the neonatal period, are spent being cared for, usually by the parents. In week three, known as the transition period, the nervous system undergoes a huge transition, and the puppy becomes a functional unit capable of receiving stimuli, reacting to them, and interacting with the environment. Week four begins the socialization period, which lasts until around week 12 and is the primary imprint period of the dog, when the puppy forms social bonds and, more important for decoys, learns what is normal in life. The things that the puppy learns are normal during this period tends to be regarded as normal for the rest of his life (barring some traumatic event). If the puppy is not exposed to something during this period, he does not learn it is normal and so will tend to be uncomfortable or even afraid of it for the rest of his life. The things the puppy learns to like during this period tend to be liked the rest of his life. The same goes for things the puppy learns to fear during this period.

Every neuron that is regularly used during the socialization period is maintained by the body and actually gains a myelin sheath that is thicker than the ones that aren't used as much, which makes it more efficient than the less-used neurons with the comparatively thinner myelin sheaths. Those neurons that are not used regularly are not maintained and gradually disappear by the end of this socialization period. The body replaces many of these cells, but not as fast as they disappear, so the overall effect is that the neural pathways involved suffer and many eventually disappear. So, all the neurons involved in receiving stimuli from the environment and responding to it when a puppy is exposed to new things are maintained, and activity in these pathways begins to feel normal to the puppy, while neurons and pathways that are not used regularly during this time period will not feel normal when they are stimulated later in life.

The socialization period is the perfect time for the puppy to learn to like everything associated with decoys. He should be allowed to watch older dogs working in aggression so he can learn that dogs always defeat decoys and that this is normal. Observational learning is very important to dogs, and you should not pass up opportunities to employ it, no matter what age the dog is. In this vein, you should introduce the puppy to training equipment—the bite rag, tug, pillow, and wedge—pleasantly, and he should learn that no matter how tough the decoy may appear at first, if the dog fights hard enough and long enough, the decoy always turns out to be a weak coward in the end. Of course, you must be cautious about when you introduce all of these items to a puppy. Around week nine, many dogs experience what is known as the primary fear period, where things that never used to bother them suddenly create a fearful response. Normally, if we ignore these "hinkey" responses (how's that for a technical term?), the puppy grows out of them and life goes on with no negative consequences. This would be a bad time, however, for a decoy to make a mistake and pressure the young dog too much, since it is easier to get a fearful reaction at this age than at any other time in the dog's life. You really shouldn't be pressuring the puppy at this age, anyway. You should not have a problem if you are teaching through observation, game playing, and food rewards, which is what you should be doing with dogs at this age.

ADULT LEARNING

Adult learning also affects behaviors. This is where the classical and operant conditioning, latent learning, and habituation you have heard about come into play. In truth, these forms of learning are operating during the socialization period, too, but it is useful to consider them separately because they continue to be in effect all through adult life, whereas the imprint process (where the dog learns what is normal and what is not) ends when the socialization period comes to a close. So, when genetics encourage the dog to exhibit a certain behavior and that behavior feels normal due to proper imprinting and socialization, the last factor to contribute is the chemical change, if any, that occurs in the brain. When the behavior results in the neurotransmitter dopamine being released into the part of the brain known as the mesolimbic reward pathway, it creates such a pleasant feeling that the dog feels rewarded and becomes motivated to repeat whatever behavior he thinks leads to that feeling. If, on the other hand, the situation results in a release of the neurotransmitter acetylcholine into the part of the brain known as the "punishment circuit," such an unpleasant feeling arises that the dog feels punished and will often try to avoid whatever he thinks led to that sensation. This will often stimulate what is known as the behavior inhibition system, which decreases the occurrence of behaviors that are undesirable in certain situations.

This system enables the dog to conform productively to things such as the rules of the pack.

When, as a decoy, you stimulate aggressive behaviors (and there are many different ones, as you will see later), you rely on genetics and the proper concentrations of brain chemicals to encourage the dog to show aggression. If you do not start with a dog that has the correct genotype to show aggressive behaviors, you are at a severe disadvantage and should search for a dog with a better genotype. In this work, you also rely on the physical development of the dog's neural pathways in the brain, which only comes about through proper socialization, or imprinting, where the puppy was pleasantly introduced to everything about the decoy and aggression and learned that this kind of training is normal. If the puppy does not recognize work with a decoy as normal, you are again at a severe disadvantage; in some cases, a dog that was not exposed to decoys and aggression work as a puppy may not ever become comfortable with it. When genetics encourages the dog to exhibit a behavior that feels rewarding—dopamine released in the reward pathway—his behavior is reinforced and is likely to be repeated. If the behavior results in a release of acetylcholine into the punishment circuit, the dog will avoid engaging in that behavior.

Remember, there are no mysterious drives accumulating units of energy that must be released and therefore forcing the dog into certain behaviors. Behaviors (including aggression) result from genetic predispositions that are either reinforced or punished; it's all about DNA, brain development, and brain chemistry—not drives.

> There are no mysterious drives accumulating units of energy that must be released and therefore forcing the dog into certain behaviors. Behaviors (including aggression) result from genetic predispositions that are either reinforced or punished; it's all about DNA, brain development, and brain chemistry—not drives.

The Types of Aggression

Studies with other species—often cats—indicate that aggression is regulated by activity in certain areas of the brain, mostly the hypothalamus and the amygdala.[4] By stimulating certain areas, scientists have been able to create two types of aggression. One seems to be connected with the gathering of food and the other with excitement of emotional responses. The food-gathering behavior (predatory aggression) can be produced by electrical stimulation of that area of the brain called the lateral hypothalamus and can be inhibited by activity in the ventromedial hypothalamus. This behavior is defined by low-key, quiet body language and stalking approaches that minimize distance-increasing signals (see chapters 3 and 4 for discussions of these). Its main purpose is the capture and death of the target animal and is characterized by bites to the neck, throat, and head.

Other types of aggression seem to involve the autonomic system, which affects heart rate, blood pressure, pupil dilation, and raised hackles (among other responses), and have been called "affective" forms of aggression. Some can be produced by electrical stimulation of the medial hypothalamus in the brain and are characterized by numerous distance-influencing signals and, in some cases, a lot of noise. The damage inflicted by an animal engaging in affective aggression is often serious, even fatal, but is not intended primarily to kill. The amygdala and the hypothalamus interact to produce the amount of aggression we see in both types of aggression (food gathering and affective).

As with many behaviors, propensity to aggression stems from the genetic makeup of the dog. Genetic factors develop and control the physical structures of the brain mentioned above. Chemicals and hormones also affect expressions of aggression. Injections of acetylcholine into the hypothalamus can produce affective forms of aggression in some species, while increased levels of serotonin in the brain seem to reduce aggressive responses. The influence of chemicals on the nervous system, particularly in regard to aggression, is not well-defined at this time. Much work is being done on the chemical basis of behavior, though, and the next 10 years should show radical increases in our knowledge of the subject. It is a topic that dog trainers should keep their eyes on.

The effect of male hormones (androgens) on aggression is well known. Androgens do not seem to influence predatory aggression, but scientists feel that the presence of androgens in the brain during puppy development increases the potential for affective aggression when the dog matures. Because of this, more males show high levels of aggression as adults than females (except when females are protecting their puppies). Unfortunately, this information has led to the belief that only intact males (with testicles) have enough aggression for police work, which is not true. Once the aggressive responses have been learned and properly maintained, a male dog can be castrated and still perform as well as before. Certain females and castrated males have strong aggressive tendencies and make good police dogs. Relying on general information usually works when dealing with large numbers of dogs, but when you work with individuals—as decoys do—remember there are always notable exceptions. If you would not judge a book by its cover, do not judge a dog by his breed, sex, size, or color. Before we launch into descriptions of the various forms of aggression, it might be useful to divide them into two categories: "affective" (of which there are 10) and "non-affective" (of which there are four).

TYPES OF CANINE AGGRESSION

AFFECTIVE
1. Territorial
2. Pain induced
3. Fear induced
4. Inter-male
5. Social (Dominance)
6. Protective
7. Maternal
8. Learned
9. Redirected
10. Irritable

NON-AFFECTIVE
1. Sexual
2. Predatory
3. Play
4. Idiopathic

TERRITORIAL

Territorial is the first form of affective aggression. It is extremely prevalent in dogs and is so important that it can reverse dominance relationships. Many dogs are much more dominant and confident in their own territory than they are somewhere else. This is why good trainers always test candidates on strange territory (police dogs rarely work at home; they are usually working on someone else's turf). The space around a dog is divided into several categories, including home range, territory, social space, and personal space (see Figure 5.1).[5]

A territory is considered to be the area the dog is willing to defend. Some dogs have such a high genetic predisposition to this

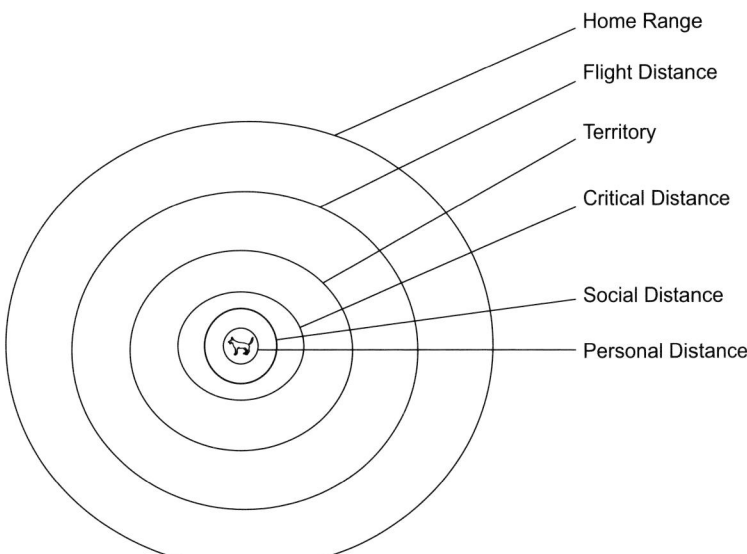

Figure 5.1 Different categories of space around the dog's body. Within their territory, dogs recognize a flight distance and a critical distance.

type of aggression that they will become aggressive the moment you cross their territorial line, regardless of what your body language is. This makes it a very useful form of aggression for police training in the initial stages of protection work. All you have to do is set the dog up in the same spot enough times for him to consider that place his territory and then physically jump back and forth across the border to stimulate aggression. In advanced stages of training, these dogs need to be taught to ignore territory completely, but this is usually done after aggression becomes a learned response and can be reliably triggered. Some dogs need encouragement (in the form of body language) to respond this way, and some are not interested in defending territory at all unless strongly provoked. The boundaries of a dog's territory can be well-defined in the form of a fence, the borders of the car he is in, or a road. However, the line is often unseen visually, which leads some people to think it is imaginary. To fully appreciate dogs, you must accept that the line is very real to them. They always seem to know exactly where it is, even though we have trouble keeping track of it.

PAIN INDUCED

Pain-induced aggression is common in practically all domestic species of animal, and the dog is no exception. Dogs have individual tolerances to pain, so the speed and severity of their reactions to it can vary from animal to animal. Pain is at the basis of an old form of stimulation known as flanking, where the decoy would approach the dog calmly, or even in a friendly manner, grasp the skin of the dog in the flank area just in front of the hind legs, and pinch and twist the skin as hard as possible before jumping back before the dog could bite. The dog would instinctively bite at the source of the pain and see that aggression could make the source of the pain go away. Some people still use this method, while some pinch the ears or the cheeks, and others use sticks or whips to get the same results. It is a fast method of bringing out aggression and works well in some dogs. However, it does not work well in a large number of dogs and is no longer recommended as a standard technique for dogs beginning training. Small children often do horrible things to dogs just out of curiosity (and usually when their parents can't see what they are doing). Infants and small children should never be left alone with working dogs. It is too easy for children to inflict pain on dogs without realizing what they are actually doing. Dogs that have been flanked will react quickly and decisively to such treatment.

Pain is also part of the basis for what many trainers erroneously refer to as the "defensive drive" of dogs. It teaches several things. First, that the proper response to pain is aggression. This is not always the case, as when a child grabs the dog's coat or ears during a public-relations demonstration. Or when your young daughter trips and falls on the dog while he is asleep. Or when the veterinarian has to handle him or give an injection. The list can go on, but the point is clear: aggression is not always the proper response to pain. Employing too much pain in training also teaches the dog that working with humans is not fun, but rather a very serious business. Triggering too much pain-induced aggression too early in a dog's training often produces a dog that has difficulty relaxing and being confident in his ability to handle any situation.

Confident dogs that have had too much pain-induced aggression triggered will give ambivalent signals and are easy to recognize. They look much like other confident, aggressive dogs except they show a lot of lip curl and snarling along with raised hackles and the stiff, tense, leg movements described in chapter 3 as signs of minor insecurity. Insecure dogs that have too much pain-induced aggression triggered appear just like other insecure, aggressive dogs and are fear biters. So, the ability to handle pain-induced aggression must be developed carefully in dogs. Too much emphasis on it creates dogs of limited value. While they can complete basic assignments, they often become too stressed out to be good at the advanced levels of service-dog training. Consequently, many trainers prefer to begin working with other forms of aggression first, leaving work on pain-induced aggression for later in training.

After the dog has learned confidence through less-stressful methods, such trainers start triggering pain-induced aggression, but just enough to create balance between it and the other forms.

The third thing that flanking and other painful techniques teach is that humans cannot be trusted. They will often approach in a friendly manner, but this is a ruse to set you up for an attack. Consequently, dogs should not let humans approach them. This is a two-edged sword. Some handlers prefer a dog that no one—except the handler—can approach (most of them work in bad areas of cities where, admittedly, the environment is more hostile than it is for many other officers). These handlers seem to be in the minority now, though, as most officers see unapproachable dogs as an unnecessary liability. Instead, most officers prefer dogs that are approachable and safe when the officer–dog team has to interact with the public. As a result, the dog's ability to handle pain-induced aggression should be accomplished carefully and always in balance with the other forms of aggression. If it becomes the primary focus of training, you will limit the dog when he comes to the advanced levels of training and in many cases expose yourself to unnecessary liabilities.

> **The dog's ability to handle pain-induced aggression should be accomplished carefully and always in balance with the other forms of aggression. If it becomes the primary focus of training, you will limit the dog when he comes to the advanced levels of training and in many cases expose yourself to unnecessary liabilities.**

Pain-induced aggression also causes trouble when painful techniques are used to teach aggression control. When pain is used to punish aggression to make it decrease or go away completely, and the dog has a genetic predisposition to respond aggressively to pain, the punishment will actually increase the aggression, not make it go away. The more pain you use, the more the dog will hold on and bite harder, even though you want the dog to let go—and it is your fault. By inflicting pain on a dog with a predisposition for pain-induced aggression, you have increased his aggression levels and forced him to behave badly. He had no choice. Using pain as punishment to make the dog cease aggression and release the decoy relies on what is known as an "escape reaction." Many years ago, most of the dogs decoys trained had low tolerances for pain and the old methods based on punishment worked quite well. It was easy to inflict enough pain to trigger an escape reaction since the pain was so unpleasant the dog would stop anything to escape it. Most of the dogs we see in training now are not like that. They have much higher pain tolerances, and it is physically difficult to inflict enough pain to cause an escape reaction. So, we are seeing an increase in the use of multiple pinch collars, sharpened pinch collars, and even multiple electronic collars in an effort to inflict enough pain. In most cases when using such apparatus, all we see is a dog that screams and bites harder: we have increased the pain level but still not enough necessary for an escape reaction. The obvious answer for dogs such as these is to teach aggression control with methods that do not rely on pain or an escape reaction for effectiveness. Some of these methods are explained in one of my other books, *Aggression Control: Teaching the Out* (Brush Education, 2009).

FEAR INDUCED

Fear-induced aggression is a response to something that frightens the dog. Many dogs do not have the genetic makeup to withstand threats or pressure. They will do their best to submit to the frightening object or animal, but if these attempts do not remove the fear of the situation, they resort to other measures. When the threat reaches the flight distance (see Figure 5.1), dogs escape if that is physically possible. If flight is not an option, and the threat keeps approaching, they will take action when the threat reaches the critical distance (see Figure 5.1). Passive and submissive dogs will lie down, roll over, and hope for mercy. Others seem to make the decision that it is time to fight, even though they don't want to. This is the classic fear biter, bane of all veterinarians and kennel workers. If given the chance, fear biters would much rather escape than fight. But if they see no way out, they will fight with ferocity, doing whatever damage is necessary to make the fear go away. That is the key: remember that fear is the root of this type of aggression. Remove the fear and the aggression will disappear. This kind of triggering method has similarities to pain-induced aggression because sometimes it is the fear of pain that the dog is reacting to. However, sometimes the dog is frightened of something that has never inflicted pain on him, so we cannot call this pain-induced aggression.

Neophobia (the fear of new or strange things) can trigger this type of aggression, as can startling confrontations in which no contact is made but in which the dog is taken by surprise. Decoys who use signals or approaches that are too strong for a dog can drive the dog into this type of aggression by mistake. This is usually an error and the sign of a low-quality decoy if it happens frequently. Fear-induced aggression is another part of what some trainers erroneously call the dog's "defensive drive," so it should be used as carefully as anything else connected to this defensive drive (review the cautions listed under pain-induced aggression; most of them apply to fear-induced aggression, too). Many people think dogs with high levels of fear-induced aggression make good police dogs. This is not usually true. The classic fear biter will often break and run when given the chance and is not a reliable protector. Instead, he is mostly interested in feeling less afraid, and escape will accomplish that.

INTER-MALE

Inter-male aggression is restricted to male-to-male conflict. It is not general competition for rank in the pack, which can involve females, but aggression shown by a male dog specifically aimed at another male dog. It is never directed at females. It is the source of much of the dog-fighting problems trainers encounter and as such is not terribly useful to police-dog trainers. A dog should be tested for a proclivity for inter-male aggression before he enters training.

SOCIAL

Social aggression (sometimes referred to as dominance aggression) serves to maintain order in the pack. It is the mechanism by which disagreements regarding social rank are ultimately settled. There are two basic types of dominant dogs. The first is what I call passively dominant, in that he does not consider any other animal to be higher ranking, but sees no reason to fight for dominance. The passively dominant dog tends to ignore most signs of disrespect from others but will not show respect for anyone else, either. In some instances, it is easy to mistake this kind of dominant dog for a low-ranking dog, until it is too late. The other is what I call actively dominant: a dog that immediately seeks a leadership position when placed among a strange group of dogs (and will fight to attain it), responds actively to any challenge by a lower-ranking dog, and will let no sign of disrespect go unanswered. The actively dominant dog often shows a high level of social aggression, which is part of what many trainers erroneously call "fight drive," since these dogs will fight any time they don't get exactly what they want. After all, the rules of the dog world seem to be that dominant animals get everything they want. Any lower-ranking dog that doesn't give them exactly what they want deserves to be punished. Social aggression is an extremely useful form of aggression for police-dog trainers. All they have to do is to convince the dog that the handler and maybe one other person are the top-ranking animals, that the dog comes next, and that everyone else in the world is below them in rank. The dog will then obey the handler (and one other person in case the handler is ever down or incapacitated) but instantly fight anyone else in the world at the handler's bidding. When this kind of dog fights, he displays confident body language.

> Social aggression is an extremely useful form of aggression for police-dog trainers.

PROTECTIVE

Protective aggression can be confused with social aggression. Sometimes dominant dogs fight to maintain possession of something, but this behavior is really a way of defending rank. Protective aggression can also occur in lower-ranking dogs that are not trying to take a leadership position. They select something and protect it while making no efforts to increase their social position. Sometimes such dogs protect another dog, sometimes a human, and sometimes an object. Dogs that are bred for and participate in Ringsport perform an exercise where they must guard strange, unknown objects selected at random by the judge. As a result, Ringsport dogs can be strongly predisposed to this type of aggression due to their breeding, which makes it very difficult on occasion to get their toys back from them. Sometimes such dogs consider the decoy their favorite toy and refuse to give him up, causing aggression-control problems. (Ideas on how to approach this are beyond the scope of this book, but you could look at one my other books, *Aggression Control: Teaching the Out*, for suggestions.) However, this form of aggression is useful in some dogs whose other forms of aggression are poorly developed but that have a favorite person. Sometimes they will show aggression to protect their handlers but not to defend themselves or gather food. As such, it is a useful form of aggression, but many trainers feel it should be strongly supported by other types.

MATERNAL

When a bitch protects her puppies, she is engaging in maternal aggression. Many think the male is more aggressive than the female, but this is not the case, especially considering maternal aggression. Normally friendly bitches can be transformed when they have puppies. They become some of the most aggressive animals you will ever meet. It pays to be careful around first-time mothers until you get some idea of how they are coping with the new experience. One of the more interesting versions of this type of aggression occurs when a bitch is pseudo-pregnant; she is not pregnant but has a hormonal imbalance that makes her think she is. She will often pick an object, such as a shoe or sock, and treat it as if it were a puppy. In some cases, she will even produce milk for the chosen object. If you try to get your shoe or sock back, she may react with severe maternal aggression. While all of this is interesting, maternal aggression has no real value in training police dogs.

LEARNED

Learned aggression can begin like any of the other forms. Once the aggression has been sufficiently rewarded and maintained, it becomes a learned response and no longer requires the original stimuli to trigger it, merely a cue from the handler or the decoy. Sometimes, however, the dog becomes aggressive with no cue from the humans and because of a reward that occurs by accident. This causes problems for pet owners, but learned aggression is quite prevalent in police-dog training. In fact, most of what we teach becomes learned at some point.

REDIRECTED

Redirected aggression occurs when another form of aggression cannot be expressed. For instance, when the dog really wants to bite a dominant dog (or person) but does not dare to do so. In such cases, he frequently redirects the aggression to a lower-ranking dog and bites him instead of the dominant dog (that originally triggered the aggression). Frequently, the recipient will turn and take it out on the next dog down the line, and so on. This type of aggression can be observed when handlers irritate dogs using painful techniques to gain control during protection work, which is one of the major problems of that approach to control. The dog doesn't really want to bite his master but is being stimulated, so he redirects the aggression to the nearest animal of lower rank, the decoy. Instead of sitting and barking, as desired by the handler, for example, he will run in and take a dirty bite (or perhaps refuse to release the decoy if he is already biting) to avoid getting into real trouble by biting his handler. One of the best approaches to this problem is for handlers and decoys to teach control without using painful techniques (see *Aggression Control: Teaching the Out*).

IRRITABLE

Irritable aggression occurs when something irritates the dog enough to make him aggressive. Mostly, these dogs just want to be left alone. The source of the irritation usually goes away, which rewards the dog for such behavior. It is more likely to occur when dogs are sick or hungry and less tolerant of disturbances. As we saw in the last paragraph, excited dogs that are intent on doing something and have an incompetent handler can become irritated enough to bite. Dogs are more prone to irritable aggression when they are older than they were as younger dogs. This type of aggression can be a problem in retired service dogs that are less tolerant of nuisances and have had extensive bite training. Generally, this is not a useful type of aggression for police work, but decoys can fuss with dogs that have high levels of irritable aggression by rubbing the hair on their faces against the grain and doing other annoying things until they snap at them. With enough reward, irritable aggression can become a type of learned aggression, but often it is not worth the time invested.

SEXUAL

Sexual aggression is the first form of non-affective aggression. It is related directly to mating. Often the female is not receptive and wants the male to leave her alone. If he doesn't, she will become aggressive to make her point. Sometimes the male will become aggressive to maintain control of a receptive female. In essence, any aggression that is connected to the act of mating is considered sexual aggression. It is generally not a useful form of aggression for police-dog training.

PREDATORY

Many scientists consider this form of non-affective aggression merely a form of food-gathering behavior. Nonetheless, it is extremely useful in training police dogs. This is a low-stress type of aggression, where the dog chases a small, non-threatening animal that runs away from him. If the dog chooses the correct sort of prey, there is not much of a fight at the end of the chase and nothing to be frightened of. This is the basis of what some trainers call the "prey drive" in dogs. It gives a dog the desire to chase decoys and apprehend them, once the dog is confident in his ability to beat decoys. As such, it is a crucial aspect of police-dog training. However, training this type of aggression should not be overemphasized. For instance, it is possible to train sport dogs to score highly in competition manwork using only predatory aggression. The dogs become what we call "sleeve happy" and have no intention of getting into a real fight.

If predatory aggression has been overemphasized in a dog's training, the dog will not do well on the street. The trick to training this type of aggression is to balance predatory aggression with pain-induced, fear-induced, and social aggression so that the dog is strong in all three (the so-called prey, defense, and fight drives). Some sport trainers do this and some do not. This is why some sport dogs can be easily converted to police dogs and some cannot. It all depends on their genetic makeup and how their first trainers developed aggression in them. Predatory aggression is also one of the problems that many pet dogs have with children. Children have quick, jerky movements, love to squeal like prey species and run away, and are about the right size to be considered prey objects. As I've already mentioned, infants and small children should never be left alone with working dogs. They are masters at triggering aggression in dogs. I often tell decoy candidates to study the movements and actions of children. Children are the best natural decoys in the world, unfortunately.

PLAY

Play aggression allows young dogs to practice adult fighting skills—important later in life—without having to hurt each other.

In young adults, this type of aggression is still present, but one of the participants nearly always begins the fight by performing Bekoff's play bow. Once that signal is given, so everyone involved understands that what follows is play, some of the most ferocious-looking things can happen, but all bites are inhibited and no damage results. This kind of fighting can scare the daylights out of owners, but it is apparently quite entertaining for the dogs. This type of aggression can also be useful in police-dog training when we make mistakes. For instance, when a decoy triggers too much defensive aggression in a young dog there can be confidence problems. One way a decoy can alleviate the problem caused is to play bow to the dog, suggesting that the dog misunderstood him and that what just happened was actually play. After a certain amount of play-type aggression, the dog's confidence will return, and the decoy can again direct him to the more serious, defensive aggression in a later training session.

IDIOPATHIC

The last form of non-affective aggression is difficult to categorize and is listed here because I'm not quite sure where else it belongs. Idiopathic aggression is that which has no known or definable origin. The origin exists, we just don't know what it is. Many times it is caused by a tumor somewhere in the nervous system or brain. Sometimes it is triggered by a chemical imbalance in the brain. Often the cause cannot be determined until the dog has died and a necropsy can be performed. Dogs affected by this type of aggression are usually unpredictable and extremely dangerous to work with. Their aggression cannot be controlled reliably, and you never know what might trigger an aggressive reaction. Sometimes there is no triggering stimulus that we can identify. This type of aggression is of no use to police-dog trainers. Dogs showing this type of aggression should be eliminated from police training.

The aggressive makeup of a dog is composed of many separate factors. Trainers need to balance these factors in particular mixtures to get the best possible results. For them to do this, they need decoys who can trigger individual types of aggression on demand without triggering others. When aggression-control work begins, trainers need decoys who can also quickly stop triggering any kind of aggression. This requires the decoy to have knowledge of the sort of body language that will trigger each form of aggression, not to mention the discipline to practice enough to master the subject. It takes many years to become a good decoy, as opposed to being someone who just takes bites to help out.

6

Stimulating and Rewarding Canine Aggression

In chapter 4 you learned how to present yourself as a dominant, frightening animal, or a submissive, non-threatening one. This was accomplished by using distance-increasing and distance-decreasing signals in different combinations. In the previous chapter, you learned there are 14 different types of aggression in dogs. Now it is time to combine this information by pairing the useful types of aggression with the sort of signals that stimulate them. In general, you want to remember that in the world of dogs, only upper-ranking animals are allowed to use distance-increasing signals since they are the only ones allowed to control the space around them. Consequently, distance-increasing signals are considered to be stressing, challenging, fear provoking, or mentally pressuring.

In contrast, lower-ranking or frightened dogs use distance-decreasing signals so the upper-ranking dogs know they are not challenging them or trying to control the space around themselves. Consequently, distance-decreasing signals are considered to be calming, submitting, non-threatening, or pressure releasing. To engage in a confrontation and force the opponent to release pressure with those sorts of signals seems to be extremely rewarding for dogs, so decoys often use distance-decreasing signals when they wish to reward a dog for a particularly good performance.

Many decoys find it helpful to distinguish between the bite and the reward for aggression. The two are not the same. The bite is not the major reward for aggression. It is pleasurable for some dogs, to be sure, but it is not the major reward. The bite is the tool that the dog uses to get the reward, which is usually some particular type of signal or behavior in the adversary. These signals and behaviors are specific for each type of aggression and must be supplied by the decoy for the dog to develop to her full potential.

> **The bite is not the major reward for aggression. It is pleasurable for some dogs, to be sure, but it is not the major reward. The bite is the tool that the dog uses to get the reward, which is usually some particular type of signal or behavior in the adversary. These signals and behaviors are specific for each type of aggression and must be supplied by the decoy for the dog to develop to her full potential.**

Stimulating Territorial Aggression

You can stimulate territorial aggression when you move into and out of the dog's territory or space. Dogs with strong territorial aggression don't care what type of body language you are using; it is the crossing of the border that stimulates them. Strangely enough, these dogs often don't mind you being in their territory or space half as much as they mind you crossing the border to approach them. It is sometimes better to stay farther away from them, so you can frequently jump back and forth over the line.

If the dog retains confident body language, you can use distance-increasing signals as you cross the border, but when the dog has reacted properly, you should jump back across the border, giving distance-decreasing signals. As noted before, this rewards the dog and increases her confidence. The ultimate reward for territorial aggression is for the dog to see the enemy leave the territory.

Figure 6.1 Schematic of route followed to stimulate territorial aggression.

Therefore, at the end of the session, you should run away, leaving the dog master of her territory.

Stimulating Pain-Induced Aggression

Pain-induced aggression can be stimulated with any method that inflicts pain and still allows you, the decoy, to get away safely. I describe methods of flanking in the previous chapter, where I also note that many trainers only stimulate this form of aggression after the dog has developed other, less-stressful forms. When the dog is confident and working well, you can introduce small amounts of pain with something like a light stick. Always reward the dog by running away after she shows aggression to the pain. Remember that the removal of pain is the reward for this type of aggression, not merely getting to bite. If a bite makes the pain go away, it is the bite that is rewarded, but it is the lack of pain that is the actual reinforcement.

Stimulating Fear-Induced Aggression

You can trigger fear-induced aggression when using body language that is too strong (has too many or too severe distance-increasing signals for what the dog can handle at the moment) (see Figure 6.2).

If this body language only produces a small amount of aggression in the dog, and you quickly change to distance-decreasing signals and run away, the dog will profit by learning that she need not fear humans who give such signals. Fear-induced aggression can also be stimulated by anything else that frightens the dog: you could ambush the dog, for example, by jumping out in a threatening manner when she is unprepared (for instance when she is being taken for a walk between training sessions). Trainers have used this technique for a long time to test a dog's ability to handle fearful situations. Some trainers test canine candidates in this manner and only train the survivors, while others save the technique for later in training when the dog's confidence levels are at maximum.

Both of the methods described in the above paragraph work. Anything that makes the dog suspicious will stimulate a mild form of fear-induced aggression, since suspicion is a mild form of fear.

Figure 6.2 A decoy demonstrating distance-increasing signals. (Photo by Darryl Lindsay)

STIMULATING AND REWARDING CANINE AGGRESSION

Figure 6.3 A decoy creeping suspiciously out from behind a tree. (Photo by Darryl Lindsay)

Figure 6.4 A decoy fleeing. (Photo by Darryl Lindsay)

This is why some decoys dress and move strangely until the dog alerts in their direction, and then they run away (see Figures 6.3 and 6.4).

Strange movements followed by running away are effective in suggesting the presence of something frightening and then reassuring the dog that she need not fear the strange thing after all, since one good bark will make it run away.

If only small amounts of fear are generated by the above-described techniques, and each experience concludes with the dog victorious, the dog's confidence increases. If too much fear is generated by any of these methods, the dog will become more and more insecure, and too many experiences of this type will produce a dog with too much fear-induced aggression. As noted before, these dogs are of limited use in police work since they are too stressed out for advanced maneuvers. Introducing the dog to potentially frightening situations is important in the training of a police-service dog, but it must be done carefully to avoid creating fear biters. The reward for this type of aggression is the lowering of fear levels in the dog. This can usually be accomplished by letting the dog see the frightening stimulus (the decoy) become less frightening, such as when the decoy runs away. Again, a bite is not necessarily the reward. The removal of fear is the reinforcement.

Stimulating Social Aggression

You can stimulate social aggression by establishing yourself as a lower-ranking animal and then challenging the dog's rank in the pack by displaying some distance-increasing signals. As I mentioned earlier, this violates the rules of the dog world, and it is the responsibility of the upper-ranking dog to punish the rude, lower-ranking dog (in this case, the decoy). This is one of the ways dogs maintain order and stability in the pack. If the dog has a strong predisposition to social aggression, you need only challenge her by using distance-increasing signals and she will react swiftly and strongly. If the dog has a lesser predisposition for this type of aggression, you must first give as many distance-decreasing signals as possible when interacting with the dog, which establishes you, in time, as a lower-ranking animal. This can often be achieved in one session, but with some dogs it takes multiple sessions.

Once this rank has been established, you can begin to give a few distance-increasing signals. For instance, you might actually turn and look into the dog's eyes for a second, then break eye contact and resume distance-decreasing signals (see Figures 6.5, 6.6, and 6.7).

STIMULATING AND REWARDING CANINE AGGRESSION

Figure 6.5 To stimulate social aggression, the decoy begins working the dog with distance-decreasing signals. (Photo by Darryl Lindsay)

Figure 6.6 Just for an instant, the decoy switches to distance-increasing signals. (Photo by Darryl Lindsay)

Figure 6.7 The decoy quickly returns to displaying distance-decreasing signals. (Photo by Darryl Lindsay)

If the dog does not respond, increase the number and intensity of distance-increasing signals (always followed by distance-decreasing signals to show underlying insecurity) until the dog reacts aggressively. At the first sign of aggression from the dog, run away, showing as many distance-decreasing signals as possible. Several repetitions of this will convince the dog that you, the decoy, are nothing but a rude coward who can be easily beaten. After a while, the dog will be willing to fight harder and harder to win, knowing that if she just fights long and hard enough, she can always beat you.

The reward for training this type of aggression is the establishment of the dog as the upper-ranking animal. However, the signals that show submission are also the ones that stimulate predatory aggression (see below). Consequently, by switching to the distance-decreasing signals used in predatory aggression, you can reward the dog for fighting well in social aggression. If a bite is what leads to the other animal signaling submission, then the bite is rewarded, but keep in mind that it is the signaling of submission by the adversary that is the actual reward.

Stimulating Predatory Aggression

You can stimulate predatory aggression by imitating the movements of prey animals. Most prey species run away when attacked and often give distance-decreasing signals when caught. So, objects that move quickly away from or across the front of dogs tend to stimulate this form of aggression. Often decoys tie tug toys to the ends of ropes or leashes and drag them on the ground behind them, angling slightly away from the dog to encourage her to chase after the toy and catch it. If the dog is successful, she is allowed to carry the prize around and show off a little (see Figure 6.8).

Figure 6.8 Dragging the tug in front of a dog. The stake line is pulling the dog to the left. (Photo by Darryl Lindsay)

Table 6.1 Stimulating and Rewarding Aggression

Type of Aggression	Stimulant	Reward
Pain induced	Pain	Pain reduces or goes away
Fear induced	Frightening stimulus	Frightening thing becomes less frightening
Social	Disrespectful, challenging, distance-increasing signals	Respectful, submissive, distance-decreasing signals
Predatory	Distance-decreasing signals with lots of movement	Capture of prey, cessation of movement with distance-decreasing signals, feigning death

Use distance-decreasing signals during this drill and encourage the dog to play tug-of-war before she releases the toy. Eventually, use a burlap roll and then place it on a protective sleeve, which you can allow to slip off as soon as the dog bites it. The dog then gets to carry the sleeve around to show off. Since fast movement away from the dog is actually one of the come-here signals, the maximum use of distance-decreasing signals is what stimulates predatory aggression. The reward for this type of aggression is the simulation of death by the prey object or decoy. This is why the dog so enjoys prancing around with the "dead" sleeve or tug toy in her mouth. If this is not possible, you should feign death from time to time to reward the dog.

Combining Types of Aggression

You can use combinations of the above approaches to suit the individual temperament of each dog you work. If one dog shows evidence of too much fear-induced aggression, you can switch to distance-decreasing signals and work the dog using predatory aggression. After predatory aggression has been increased to the point that it balances the fear-induced aggression, you can work the dog normally, since her stress levels will now be under control. Conversely, if a dog works completely in predatory aggression, and can't handle fear-induced aggression well, you can switch to distance-increasing signals and gradually build the fear-induced aggression of the dog to the point at which it balances with the predatory component. Again, once you reach this balance, you can work the dog normally.

Often it will be best to use both increasing and decreasing signals in the same session, as when you are working with social aggression, or the so-called "fight drive." You simply use more of the type the dog needs to develop properly. Sometimes you want to use all three types of aggression in the same workout. If you prefer to work with social aggression, but the dog also has a problem handling fear-induced aggression, you could use a mixture of signals, emphasizing the distance-increasing signals to develop the fear-induced aggression more fully. If you wish to develop predatory aggression more fully, you could use social aggression, emphasizing the distance-decreasing signals to develop predatory aggression more fully. Some trainers like to work one type of aggression for a period, bring that type to a peak, and then switch to another type and work that for a while. This switching of types in the same workout is sometimes called "channeling the dog."

Understanding which signals trigger which type of aggression gives you the ability to adjust, second by second, to what the dog needs. You simply reads the dog's body language and react with the proper signals. This is far superior to decoying in set patterns simply because that's the way you were originally taught to do it and don't know any other formula. Decoying should never be a formula. It should be a dynamic process of communication that adjusts to each dog's needs as she develops.

New decoys are frequently confused regarding the type of aggression they have stimulated when working a dog. For instance, the trainer has told them to work the dog in "fight drive" (read: stimulate more social aggression than anything else), but they are not sure if that is what they are actually doing. The keys to figuring out what type of aggression you are stimulating are 1) what signals the decoy is using and 2) the body language of the dog. If the decoy is predominantly using distance-decreasing signals and the body language of the dog indicates confidence, you are most likely seeing predatory aggression. Many trainers would erroneously say that at this point you are working the dog in "predatory drive" or simply "prey drive." If the decoy is using distance-increasing signals and the body language of the dog is completely confident, you are probably seeing social aggression. Many trainers would call this working the dog in "fight drive." If at any time you see insecurity or fear in the dog's body language, you are probably looking at fear-induced or pain-induced aggression, or some combination of both. You would then be working the dog in what many trainers erroneously call "defensive drive," or just plain "defense drive."

Your ability to know which form of aggression you have stimulated is dependent on your ability to read the dog's body language. In addition, your ability to stimulate the particular type of aggression the trainer wants is dependent upon your ability to use your own body to give the correct signals at the correct strength at the correct time.

Table 6.2 Determining Which Type of Aggression Has Been Stimulated

Decoy's Signals	Dog's Signals	Additional Dog Signals	Type of Aggression
Distance increasing	Fearful		Pain or fear induced (defense)
Distance decreasing	Fearful		Pain or fear induced (defense)
Distance increasing	Complete confidence	Noisy, loud barking; wrapping forelegs around decoy's leg or body	Social (fight)
Distance decreasing, lots of movement	Confident	Silent or quiet, low head, intense focus on movement	Predatory (prey)

> Your ability to know which form of aggression you have stimulated is dependent on your ability to read the dog's body language. Additionally, your ability to stimulate the particular type of aggression the trainer wants is dependent upon your ability to use your own body to give the correct signals at the correct strength at the correct time.

The Yerkes-Dodson Law

Nowhere is the Yerkes-Dodson Law (also called the "inverted U") more prominently displayed than in dog aggression work. Over a hundred years ago, two young psychologists named Robert M. Yerkes and John Dillingham Dodson defined the relationship between excitement and behavioral performance in humans and animals: As excitement levels increase, the performance of the animal will improve until a certain optimal level of excitement is reached. If excitement levels increase beyond that optimum point, the performance of the animal will begin to decrease again and will continue to decline the more the excitement increases, as Figure 6.9 illustrates.

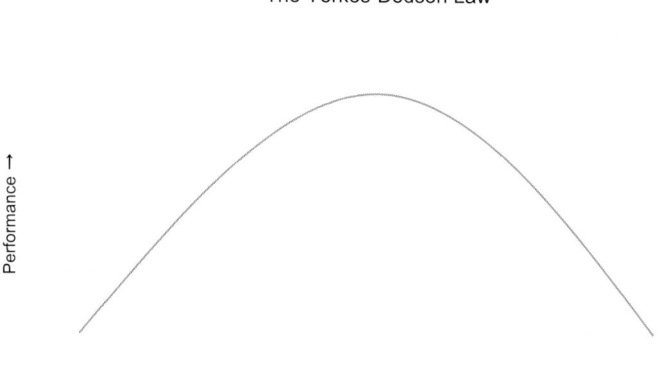

Figure 6.9 The Yerkes-Dodson Law.

As the decoy, it is your job to work the dog in whatever manner is necessary to keep the dog in the top part of the curve so that performance is maximized. Sometimes this requires you to be more exciting and sometimes this requires you to be calmer and even downright boring. Almost everyone is willing to be more exciting when necessary since most of us are excitement junkies, but very few people see the need for and are willing to be quiet and boring when that is called for. This creates difficulties in many cases, since the type of dog you are decoying can be quite different now than she was many years ago. Thirty or 40 years ago, most of the dogs taken into police training were not as excitable as the dogs that are being trained now. Consequently, the methods of decoying developed years ago emphasized building the excitement level of the dogs to maximize their performance by bringing them as far as possible up the rising left side of the Yerkes-Dodson curve. These methods and philosophies are still being taught and need to be modified to meet the needs of most of the dogs you see today. The dogs decoys see today, whether imported or domestic, are generally more excitable than the dogs decoys worked with 40 years ago, and many are performing badly because they are too excited and are on the falling, right side of the curve. These dogs need decoys to be less exciting to bring them back to the top of the curve, particularly during the learning phase of training.

Each dog needs to be evaluated individually, and you need to apply the amount of excitement appropriate for her natural excitability, which varies from dog to dog. Only when decoys do this will we see dogs reach their full potential.

7

Basic Skills

Decoys inevitably develop their own styles of working, which leads to great variation in the specific techniques that are actually employed in the field. However, if you observe enough good decoys, you will begin to see certain common denominators. While it is beyond the scope of this book to list all the different techniques used, it is useful to discuss some of the skills and items that are basic to most of them.

Safety Consciousness and the Proper Mindset

Safety consciousness is the decoy's first important skill. There are many risks involved with decoying. Some of these are avoidable; others are not. One of the most important rules of the business is: Don't take chances you don't have to. There are many risks inherent to this activity, and you take the ones you can't avoid without complaint. However, it is important to minimize the chances for injury whenever possible. Being injured decreases your ability to decoy. You let down the people who rely on you when you become injured, and the dogs also suffer. It is not a matter of courage, it is a matter of good sense and practicality. Good decoys are hard to find, and trainers cannot afford the luxury of having one injured. It's not good for you, it's not good for the trainer, and it's not good for the dog, which has to put up with mediocre decoys while you are on leave. So, do what has to be done, but don't take a chance you don't absolutely have to.

While you're at it, avoid working with decoys who have a large number of scars and seem eager to brag about them. If you don't, you will probably end up with a similar number of scars. Remember that scars are not a sign of skill. We all have some, but you should be learning the trade from someone who only has a few and doesn't consider them a reason for bragging. The quality of people you work with is critical. There is no safe way to work with a fool. No matter how careful you are, no matter how good your equipment is, a fool will find a way to get you hurt.

The first component of safety was introduced above: a mindset that emphasizes safety. Try to develop "what if" thinking. Examine each situation before you get into it, and make a mental list of all the things that could possibly go wrong. Make sure you have a reaction in mind for each possibility. Murphy's Law says that whatever can go wrong, will; Murphy's Law of Decoying says that the worst possible thing will always happen at the worst possible moment. Be ready for that at all times and you have a chance for a long and productive career. Throw caution to the wind or show off for the boys or girls and you are headed for a painful, short, but exciting year or so of decoying.

Your equipment is also important to safety. Most of the tools designed for decoying are intended to provide some measure of safety, such as groin protectors (which no one appreciates until they take a groin bite) and hand covers for use with hidden sleeves. They all have strengths and weaknesses and whether or not you use them are usually a matter of style and personal choice. There are too many devices on the market now to list them all here, but I have tried to discuss some of the common tools and their uses. Note that none of them keep you safe by themselves: Each can be used well or misused. It's how you use them that counts. Finally, a good handler and trainer make all the difference to a decoy's work and success with dogs, and to his or her ability to work safely.

MINIMAL SAFETY REQUIREMENTS FOR QUALITY DECOYING

1. Proper mindset
2. Stake line (back tie)
3. Reliable equipment
4. Proper footwear
5. Scratch pants
6. Good handler and trainer

STAKE LINE (BACK TIE)

Stake lines are not necessary pieces of equipment. Many good dogs are trained well without them, and this will continue to be the case in the future. For a new decoy, however, they are a major advantage. When I first began decoying, it was customary for the handler to hold the end of the dog's leash while the decoy worked. The trick was to get the handler to stay still. Often the dog would lunge at the decoy, pulling the handler off balance. The handler would then fall forward a step or two, and the dog would be able to make contact at a time when he shouldn't have been able to. As a result, a lot of decoys received unnecessary bites. At some point, trainers began "staking" or "back tying" the dogs, which meant that instead of being held by a human, the dog was tied in some manner to a stake or other immovable object while the decoy worked (see Figure 7.1).

Figure 7.1 With the dog securely staked to a tree, the author works safely without protective equipment. (Photo by Darryl Lindsay)

Staking thus represented a major improvement in safety. There was no human holding the line, so the decoy knew exactly how far the dog could come in his direction. As long as the dog had good motivation and the decoy drew the dog out slowly to the end of the stake line before working in earnest (so he wouldn't run forward with a slack line and hit the end of it with a bang), the stake line was quite functional and allowed the decoy to work more safely and to play tug-of-war more effectively (the dog could pull against the stake line). The stake line also eliminated some problems caused by miscommunication with the handler. No matter what happened, decoys knew exactly where they were safe and where the dog could reach them. When you use a stake line, remind the handler to push the dog out to the end of the line so it is straight and taut. That way, the dog cannot correct himself by lunging forward and hitting the end of a slack line. The longer the stake line, the more complications there are, naturally. With a long line, the dog can get tangled up more easily and the decoy can misjudge the length of the line occasionally. But even with its weaknesses, using a stake line is still safer for the decoy than employing the old method.

RELIABLE EQUIPMENT

The collars, leashes, and lines used to restrain the dog are the source of many problems. Collars fray and split, buckles separate, snaps break, leashes split, rivets fail—you name it and it can happen. Check these items before you work with a dog, and don't trust someone else to do it unless you have to. Handlers often do not appreciate the importance of decoy safety, and you should watch out for yourself whenever possible. As well, constantly monitor the condition of your protective sleeves and other equipment. A good principle to keep in mind is that anything made by humans can, and will, malfunction at some point. Equipment failure is a common cause of decoy and dog injury, and you should constantly be on guard against it. This is one of the major "what if" categories mentioned earlier.

PROPER FOOTWEAR

Many people disregard shoes when they think of safety items, but they are important to the decoy. It is difficult to decoy well or even remain safe if you slip and fall down at the wrong time. Foot movement constitutes a large part of a decoy's practice, and you need to have sure footing to do it safely. Make sure your shoes are in good repair and appropriate for the environment you are working in. For instance, cleated soccer or football shoes are best for grass fields, but these are useless inside a building, where basketball or tennis shoes are an advantage. Good decoys often bring more than one type of footwear to work.

SCRATCH PANTS

Protective trousers, often called scratch pants, are also important. Dogs are much faster than humans and usually have the advantage of acting first in a bite situation. If they elect to bite at a location on your body other than where you have tried to focus them, they have the advantage of reaction time and better overall speed. They will usually make contact before you can get out of the way. If they can't, they are not very good athletes. Adding to this the fact that some dogs like to bite legs more than anything else—and that many dogs take cheap bites as they come off the sleeve and at other times during control work; and that during realistic scenarios your legs are sometimes the only part of your body the dog can reach—it should come as no surprise that your legs get bitten from time to time.

Another factor in favor of using scratch pants is that proper sleeve presentation requires you to stand up and force the dog to come up to the sleeve to bite. This technique is a result of problems reported some years ago, where dogs trained by decoys not using scratch pants failed to bite fleeing felons because the criminals did not bend down to present the sleeve. Old-style decoys always bent down when the dog was about to bite because it was the only reliable way to keep the dogs from biting their legs. Some dogs apparently learned that if a bite was required in a situation, the person needing the bite would be bending down. They began to read a person bending down or not as a cue for when to bite and when not to. When the real criminals ran off down the street, they did not slow and bend down, so the dogs didn't bite them. Some actually ran alongside the felons, looking right at them, as if they were wondering when they would slow and bend down with the sleeve. But, they didn't bend and the dogs never bit them, allowing some to escape completely, much to the embarrassment of the K9 units.

Now we try to stand up as much as possible, making the dog come up higher to get the bite. It seems to be helping the situation. However, if you don't have scratch pants, it is hard for you to stand up straight knowing there is a good chance the dog will bite your unprotected legs. Wearing scratch pants has helped decoys stand up better, knowing that their legs are covered to some extent. This in turn has directly helped the dogs.

GOOD HANDLER AND TRAINER

One last item should be emphasized before moving on. A good handler is probably the best piece of safety equipment available to a decoy. When things go wrong, there is nothing better to have around than a competent handler who wants you to come out uninjured. Decoys are frequently saved by the skill of a good handler. As stated earlier, there is no safe way to work with a fool. They will get you into trouble, and they are often no good at getting you out.

> **There is no safe way to work with a fool. They will get you into trouble, and they are often no good at getting you out.**

Starting without Dogs

Several skills necessary for decoy work are best taught without a dog. Regardless of your decoying philosophy, there are certain steps that should always be taken in developing new decoys. Perhaps the most important thing to think about during decoy development is what to avoid. What you don't want to have happen is what was done to most of us: Put a sleeve on, be told to go out on the field to start taking bites and receive "coaching" from the sidelines. All that does is guarantee a maximum number of mistakes that will affect the dogs negatively and a maximum level of confusion or frustration for you, the unprepared decoy. So, let us examine some elementary drills that can help prepare you to meet your first dog. There is probably more than one way to accomplish this, so don't feel that you have to do exactly what you read here. Feel free to start with these drills though, since they have worked well for several years in my decoy schools and workshops.

DRILLS WITHOUT DOGS

1. Flag drills for footwork and timing
2. Sleeve-locking drills for proper presentation
3. Tape drills for bite placement
4. Sleeve-line drills for balance and figure-8 motions
5. Stick drills with sleeve line
6. Lateral-movement drills on the sleeve line

FOOTWORK AND TIMING DRILLS

The best place for new decoys to begin is with their feet. Most of the time in decoy work, you don't want to be thinking about your footwork. You have a lot of other things to worry about, and you need your feet to take care of themselves. When you are stimulating territorial aggression or doing civil agitation (working the dog with no protective equipment), you need to be able to jump in and out of the dog's space or territory whenever you wish and with such good timing that you don't get bitten.

To develop this kind of footwork in student decoys, I play a game of flags with them, dividing them into pairs, with one playing the dog's role and the other that of the decoy. They can switch roles from time to time so each gets an equal amount of work in both roles. Place two flags or cloth strips in the decoy's belt, one

BASIC SKILLS 89

Figure 7.2 Gary Hellmers and the author set up to illustrate the flag game. (Photo by Darryl Lindsay)

on each hip, and then connect the student playing the part of the dog to a stake line (usually we tie it around the waist), and have him or her get down on hands and knees to imitate the position of a dog (see Figure 7.2).

Mark the semicircle that describes how far out the "dog" can reach toward the "decoy," and then mark a second semicircle just inside that curve. The drill is then to have the "decoy" approach the "dog" and touch the inner semicircle with one foot while moving laterally in front of the "dog." The trick is to do this without the "dog" being able to grab one of the flags. This requires good footwork, speed, and timing (see Figure 7.3).

We repeat this drill several times in my decoy schools, and to create some motivation, I usually add the following rule: At the end of each pass, one of the two students does three push-ups. If the "dog" has a flag in hand, the "decoy" does the push-ups. If the "dog" has no flag and the "decoy" touched the inner circle with his or her foot, the "dog" does the push-ups. If the "decoy" fails to touch the inner semicircle with one foot, naturally, he or she does the push-ups regardless of the outcome (see Figure 7.4).

Figure 7.3 After touching the marker with his feet, the author jumps back just in the nick of time. (Photo by Darryl Lindsay)

Figure 7.4 Somebody always does push-ups. (Photo by Darryl Lindsay)

After several repetitions, students are eager to avoid the push-ups. (Bear in mind that anyone who is not healthy enough to safely do three push-ups should not be in decoy training. If there is an exception to this, you can adjust the penalty accordingly.) Those playing the decoys are also eager to improve their footwork. To this game I add drills where the decoy picks a straight line to run that will intersect with and actually allow the "dog" to take a flag (see Figure 7.5), thereby teaching my students approach angles, as well.

Figure 7.5 The "decoy" allowing the flag to be taken while practicing approach angles. (Photo by Darryl Lindsay)

SLEEVE PRESENTATION AND BITE PLACEMENT

The next thing I work on with my students is sleeve presentation and bite placement. Still working in human–"dog" pairs as described above, the "decoys" are fitted with an external sleeve and required to hold it in front of them with the thumbs of their sleeve hand held as tightly as possible to their navels and the outer sharp edge of the same hand facing out and slightly down toward the "dog's" mouths (see Figure 7.6). The "decoys" then must hold their sleeve still while running approach patterns in front of the "dog." When the "decoys" can do this properly, they can begin to move their sleeve arms naturally, provided they can lock them into position whenever I call for it.

How rough an approximation this is of where the dog will bite is not the issue. The purpose of this drill is to introduce the idea of bite placement and show student decoys that things can be done

Figure 7.6 A "decoy" practicing holding the sleeve still during approach-angle drills. (Photo by Darryl Lindsay)

to affect it without jamming the dog in the mouth. This drill has been very successful in teaching the movements and ideas needed for this particular concept.

TAPE DRILLS FOR BITE PLACEMENT

The next step in this exercise is to give the "dog" some sticky tape—masking or duct tape—rolled up into a ball, sticky side out. As the "decoy" passes in front, the "dog" is to lunge straight forward and push the tape onto the sleeve (see Figure 7.7). Wherever the tape ball lands approximates (somewhat roughly) the location on the sleeve where a real dog would have bitten. The next step is for the "decoy" to move the sleeve arm during the passes in such a way that the "dog" places the tape in particular spots on the sleeve. The "decoy" must do this without making motions that would jam a dog in the mouth. It doesn't hurt at this point to ask the "decoy" to hold the sleeve a few inches away from the body and pull it back in when the "dog" hits the sleeve with the tape. This encourages catching the dog by absorbing some of the shock rather than jamming the dog in the mouth. The "decoy" should be able to

BASIC SKILLS 93

Figure 7.7 The "dog" placing the tape ball onto the sleeve during the tape drill. (Photo by Darryl Lindsay)

Figure 7.8 Tape placed on mid-forearm. (Photo by Darryl Lindsay)

move the sleeve so that the "dog" can push the tape ball forward until it makes contact with the wrist, in the middle of the forearm, and near the elbow, depending on the instructor's wishes (see Figures 7.8 and 7.9). Then, the "decoy" can catch the tape in the correct position. It is vitally important to have each student do these

Figure 7.9 Tape placed near the elbow. (Photo by Darryl Lindsay)

drills with both arms, unless physical problems prevent it. A decoy who can place bites on either arm is much more valuable than one who can only do it on one side.

Purely for amusement, I sometimes add the push-up rule to the placement of the tape, although the "dogs" tend to cheat, which makes it quite difficult for the "decoys."

WORKING THE SLEEVE

Working the dog on the sleeve is the next step. The students should still be working in human–"dog" pairs. The "decoy" fits the sleeve with a small rope or leash so that the "dog" can grab it and pull on the sleeve (see Figure 7.10). The "dog" stops the "decoy" by taking hold of the sleeve leash and pulling the "decoy" forward and from side to side (see Figure 7.11). While the "dog" is doing this, the "decoy" is required to work the sleeve slowly and gently by moving the wrist in small figure-8 motions (see Figure 7.12). This exercise teaches student decoys to keep on balance, even when the dog is tugging in different directions, as well as to work the dog in a safe manner. Instructors will introduce other patterns of sleeve

BASIC SKILLS 95

Figure 7.10 A sleeve equipped for the sleeve-working drill. (Photo by Darryl Lindsay)

Figure 7.11 The "dog" grabbing the balance line. (Photo by Darryl Lindsay)

motion later, but the figure-8 motion is safe for the dog and simple for beginners to learn.

Before the acceptance of hard sleeves, bite bars, and the like, decoys used to do some pretty wild things with the dogs on their

Figure 7.12 The "decoy" trying to maintain footing and balance while working a figure-8. (Photo by Darryl Lindsay)

sleeves. We used to thrash the dog up and down, picking him up off the ground and then spinning around, swinging the dog (still biting the sleeve) through the air. Eventually, we began to realize that some dogs were sustaining neck injuries from these activities and others were snapping canine teeth and absorbing other oral damage. So, we started to get more conservative in our decoying styles. Part of the problem at the time was that we were often training dogs with less natural aggression than we would have liked. The dogs needed more stimulation when on the sleeve to give us the amount of fight we wanted from them. Consequently, we developed the habit of working in a wild, stimulating manner to keep the dogs at an acceptable level of aggression. We were also routinely using softer sleeves—soft and hard sleeves have the same infrastructure, but the older-style sleeves have soft padding and more padding on the inside, hence the name "soft sleeve." There was much less chance of tooth damage with such equipment. As we got better at selecting dogs with higher levels of aggression, we came to need harder sleeves—made with leather and harder materials—to protect our arms, but we still were operating with the habits of soft-sleeved decoys. This created some problems until we learned to adjust to dogs that didn't need as much stimulation and could actually hurt themselves on hard sleeves.

The idea now is to select dogs with natural forms of aggression, catch them well, and work with conservative, small, slow movements when they are on the sleeve (even when using a soft sleeve). The figure-8 motion is the preferred pattern at this time.

ABSORBING CONCUSSION

Many dogs are so eager to fight the decoy that they charge into him or her too fast for their own good, creating severe concussions that result in injury both to themselves and the decoy. It is therefore valuable for you to develop the habit of reducing concussion whenever possible. In drills where you are moving away from the dog, concussion is automatically reduced, but sometimes you are stuck in a position where you cannot move away from the dog. One way to reduce concussion in this situation is to let the dog spin you so the force of contact is dispersed into the spin. I teach my students how to do this by having the "decoy," sleeve presented, face the person playing the part of the dog, and I then have the "dog" charge into the sleeve. When the "dog" makes contact, the "decoy" steps back with the appropriate foot, allowing the "dog" to spin him or her around. This is a useful trick to have up your sleeve when you have room on both sides to allow for spinning, but sometimes you are in such a narrow space that this is not possible. There is another way to absorb a concussion if you find yourself in a tight spot. A good drill for this situation is to have the "decoy" face the "dog" with sleeve presented and the foot on the same side as the sleeve placed forward toward the "dog." Again, have the "dog" charge into the sleeve, and just as contact is made, the "decoy" steps back with the lead foot so far that it takes the rear position. This movement creates backward motion of the decoy's body and therefore the sleeve, and can absorb as much concussion as is possible in a narrow place.

STICK WORK

If I know a student decoy will be required to perform stick work, or if I simply want to train all my students for it just in case they have to do it someday, I introduce stick work to drills at this stage. Tie the sleeve leash or line to something solid, in the manner of a stake line. With the stick in the non-sleeve hand, the student decoy can practice hitting the line, which should be stretched tight (see Figure 7.13). This should be kept up until the student is able to make full striking motions with good speed, coming within a half inch of the line but not touching it. Then the student should run around the semicircle doing it. When proficient at this, small balloons can be taped to the line. Decoys can then practice striking them without bursting them.

Figure 7.13 The decoy practicing stick work, substituting a long-handled whip for a stick. (Photo by Darryl Lindsay)

MOVING THE DOG

In decoy work, sometimes you need to move the dog to a different location or to just move around with the dog while he is on the sleeve. When doing this, take care not to step on the dog's feet. A good drill to help student decoys learn to avoid stepping on the dog begins with tying a long line to a sleeve and securing the other end to a solid object. Sleeve on, the students can then step gently backward until the line is tight. Keeping the line snug, the students can practice moving left and right, paying close attention to their feet. When moving away from the sleeve (for example, when the sleeve is on the left arm and the students are moving to the right, or away from the sleeve), students can simply turn away from their sleeve, putting it on their hip, and walk or run normally, since when moving in this direction and a dog is on the sleeve, his feet will be far away from the decoy's feet. When moving toward the sleeve (for example, when the sleeve is on the left arm and the decoy is moving to the left, or toward the sleeve), more caution is necessary since the dog's feet are now much closer to the decoy's feet. When moving in this direction, it is safer for new decoys to side-step carefully without crossing the feet over. With more experience, decoys can learn to run in both directions—but, again, that only comes with time and experience.

Stick use should be coordinated with the direction of travel. When moving toward the sleeve, use distance-increasing signals that are challenging or potentially frightening for the dog. This is when it makes sense to use the stick to increase the challenge or fear level. When moving away from the sleeve, you turn sideways and are essentially running away from the dog, giving distance-decreasing (submissive) signals. Using the stick to increase the challenge or fear level at this time would not be useful in most circumstances and downright confusing in others. So, the general rule is to use the stick when you are moving toward the sleeve and to avoid using it when you are moving away from the sleeve.

Wrap-Up

When you are proficient at the types of drills mentioned in this chapter, you are ready to meet your first dog. You will have some idea how to judge distance and speed approaching a dog and which angles to use when doing so, how to absorb some of the shock of impact, how to place a bite where it is wanted on the sleeve, how to avoid jamming the dog in the mouth, and how to stay standing up and work the dog after he makes contact. And you learned all of this without having had the slightest chance of hurting a dog. The drills I mention above will help you have a much higher probability of success with your first encounter with a dog, thus building your confidence and allowing you to enjoy the work. It bears mentioning that your success will also be appreciated by the dogs you encounter.

8

Common Procedures

It is beyond the scope of this book to list all the possible procedures that decoys use in the course of their careers. It is more practical to describe some of the more common procedures. This will provide a uniform starting point; more advanced procedures can be added at a later time under the direct supervision of a competent instructor. By practicing these basic procedures, you will learn enough to be useful to any trainer. Use these procedures as a foundation on which to build your own personal style, adding trainer needs as you go.

Civil Agitation

Civil agitation is a term used for work done with the dog on a stake line or held by a handler. During this type of work, the decoy doesn't wear protective equipment. The goal is to stimulate the dog to try to bite the decoy when the decoy is dressed normally, but not to actually let it happen. For this work, you use whatever body signals are necessary to trigger the type of aggression the trainer wants to work with, as well as a lot of fancy footwork (like that used in the flag drill in the previous chapter) to tantalize the dog and get back out of the way before she makes contact. Civil agitation can be used at different stages in a dog's training but is always risky for you, the decoy. This is one of the risks that needs to be taken, but be sure everything else is working, ensuring as much safety as possible.

Sack or Tug Work

Other procedures are specifically designed to encourage contact between the decoy and the dog. New or young dogs are often started with "sack work." This is a phase where you stimulate whatever form of aggression is appropriate for the dog (see chapters 4, 5, and 6 for a discussion of this) and build her frustration to a pitch. When the trainer feels that the time is right for the dog to actually bite something, you present her with a rolled-up burlap sack, other rolled-up fabric, or a tug toy. You carry the sack with you for several sessions before you actually allow her to bite. During those sessions, you focus the dog on the sack by repeatedly dangling it within her reach and then pulling it back out of reach just before she can catch it. It is important to move the sack toward the dog slowly and pull it back fast, not the reverse. Merely hitting the dog in the face with the sack does not work well in many cases. By moving the sack, more than anything else, you can get the dog to pay so much attention to it that she hardly notices anything else. During this time, you use the appropriate body signals to trigger whatever type of aggression the trainer wants to work with. You often present the sack to the dog at the end of a pass, as you switch direction.

Hold the sack in the hand nearest the dog, and as you turn toward her to change direction, swing the sack firmly into the dog's mouth, placing it as far back as possible (see Figures 8.1, 8.2, and 8.3). When the dog bites it, you have to act appropriately, depending on which type of aggression the trainer is trying to develop. If predatory aggression is the object, for example, you would play a momentary game of tug-of-war, letting the dog rip the sack out of your hand, continuing to use distance-decreasing signals, and run off.

COMMON PROCEDURES

Figure 8.1 After carefully approaching a young dog, the decoy prepares to place the sack. (Photo by Laurie Mackenzie)

Figure 8.2 The decoy carefully placing the sack. (Photo by Laurie Mackenzie)

Figure 8.3 The dog getting a little tug-of-war before winning the sack. (Photo by Laurie Mackenzie)

A variation on this procedure for dogs that only have predatory aggression, and rather low levels of that, is to tie the sack onto the end of a leash or line. You then drag it behind you like a trolling fisherman. This decreases pressure by increasing the distance between you and the dog, and it allows the sack to strongly imitate the height and movement of prey animals. The dog is held on leash by the handler and allowed to chase after the sack in a straight-line pursuit (see Figure 8.4). When the trainer decides it is time for the dog to bite, run slowly enough to let the dog make contact. The brief tug-of-war can be conducted using the line so you never have to come close to the dog (see Figure 8.5).

Figure 8.4 A young dog chasing a tug on a line. (Photo by Laurie Mackenzie)

Figure 8.5 After catching the tug, the decoy and dog play tug-of-war before the dog wins the tug. (Photo by: Laurie Mackenzie)

Gradually you decrease the distance between yourself and the dog until the dog is doing normal predatory aggression work. Getting back to the normal type of sack presentation, if the trainer is trying to use social aggression, you alternate distance-increasing and -decreasing signals while playing tug-of-war (see Figure 8.6 and 8.7), before you finally admit defeat, drop the sack, and run away.

If the trainer is trying to trigger fear-induced aggression, you use as many severe distance-increasing signals as the dog can tolerate while playing tug-of-war (see Figure 8.8) before finally dropping the sack and running off.

Whatever type of aggression the trainer wants you to trigger, sack placement and tug-of-war are important. When you put the sack in the back of the dog's mouth, you teach her that she has

Figure 8.6 Tug-of-war, using distance-increasing signals. (Photo by Darryl Lindsay)

Figure 8.7 Tug-of-war, using distance-decreasing signals. (Photo by Darryl Lindsay)

Figure 8.8 Tug-of-war, using severe distance-increasing signals. (Photo by Darryl Lindsay)

more power when she uses her entire mouth (i.e., you encourage her to use a full-mouth bite). Tug-of-war helps develop the dog's jaw muscles, much as exercise strengthens any other set of muscles. It is amazing how hard a dog can bite after a good program of tug-of-war.

Recently, many trainers have found the wedge to be an efficient tool for building the bite, and decoys use it in much the same manner as the sack.

External Sleeves

The new dog often graduates to soft external sleeves after she has worked successfully with a burlap sack, tug, or wedge. Sometimes you have to tie the sack around the sleeve to bridge the mental gap, but many times the dog will bite a sleeve the first time she sees one (particularly if she has strong aggressive tendencies). Harder sleeves can be introduced next to protect the decoy. External sleeve work is merely an extension of the drills I describe in chapter 7. The decoy uses the same angles of approach, sleeve presentation, bite placement, balance, and figure-8 sleeve motion as in the drills with people playing dogs. It will help some dogs if they are focused on the sleeve—you encourage this much in the same way you help a dog to focus on a burlap sack. If you place the sleeve within her reach, always removing it just before the dog can get it, she will pay attention to little else until she can get the prize.

When you play this game to help focus the dog on the sleeve, you play it mostly with your feet, moving close enough for a bite and then jumping back just in time to prevent it. Making the sleeve the most interesting object around helps some dogs tremendously. Once the dog is focused, you can present the sleeve and allow her to bite. Then, be sure to slowly draw the dog out to the end of the stake line before working hard (to prevent the dog banging into the end of the line), and remember to change direction just before presenting the sleeve (see Figure 8.10). This change of direction places the dog slightly behind your motion, making it easier for her to get a good bite. This move is often referred to as "cocking the dog."

Once the dog is on the sleeve, step gently backward as far as necessary to keep the line snug or as close to it as the dog can handle (see Figures 8.9, 8.10, 8.11, and 8.12). This way, if something goes wrong, safety is within one step. Some trainers like to start the Bark and Hold procedure at this stage, where the dog must learn to sit and bark if the decoy is not moving. Not all trainers do this, but the ones who do like to neutralize the dog before she goes too far in her training. If your trainer is one of this number, he or she will ask you to walk up and stand motionless, directly in front of the dog. When the dog sits and barks, you reward her by moving to the side and presenting the sleeve, just as you do in the final stage of the other approaches, allowing the dog to bite. The dog eventually learns to sit and bark if you are motionless, anticipating the bite and getting her reward. When the dog is good at this, she is said to be "neutralized" (see Figure 8.13).

Figure 8.9 The author approaching the dog. (Photo by Laurie Mackenzie)

Figure 8.10 Planting the foot to reverse direction and present the sleeve. (Photo by Laurie Mackenzie)

Figure 8.11 Just after initial contact. (Photo by Laurie Mackenzie)

Figure 8.12 The decoy slowly moving backward to snug up the stake line. (Photo by Laurie Mackenzie)

Figure 8.13 The decoy and dog in position for "neutralizing." (Photo by Darryl Lindsay)

Bear in mind that at this stage of decoying, you will notice that some dogs with lower levels of aggression need help holding onto the sleeve. One way to encourage them to stay on the sleeve is to rotate the wrist of your sleeve arm back and forth in small motions after the dog has taken a bite. The rotations should be small but fast, at once producing a form of vibration in the sleeve while not making it difficult to hold. This movement imitates the wriggling of a prey animal and encourages the dog to bite harder to hold it. As the dog becomes better at holding on, you can stop vibrating the sleeve and lean back and play tug-of-war with the sleeve. Since the dog is on the stake line and the line is already tight, fear of losing the sleeve will encourage many dogs to bite harder.

When you are proficient on the stake line, introduce short pursuits to your routine. The distances can be increased as balance is mastered, until you are covering as much territory as is wished by the trainer.

Dropping the External Sleeve

A major part of external sleeve work, and a tricky topic, is the dropping of the sleeve. This is when you deliberately let go of the sleeve, allowing it to slip off your arm when running away (for this reason, this move is often referred to as "slipping the sleeve"). It is a form of reward for the dog and is used frequently with new or young dogs. Everyone agrees that young dogs like to pull the sleeve off the decoy and enjoy running around with it in their mouths (see Figure 8.14). The controversy arises when we consider how often this should be done. If you do this too often (how much this is will vary from dog to dog), you may encourage the dog to become "sleeve happy," a condition where the dog learns that the object of the game is to bite the sleeve not the man.

It is possible for sport trainers to increase a dog's scores on the competition field by deliberately focusing the dog on the sleeve. So sleeve-happy dogs can be quite successful in the sport world and at the same time offer their owners limited liability, since they literally will not bite a human, only sleeves. Other sport trainers

Figure 8.14 A dog parading with a dropped, or slipped, sleeve. (Photo by Darryl Lindsay)

want a dog that will actually protect them, and so they don't drop the sleeve very often at all, preferring to focus the dog on the man. So, within the ranks of sport competitors, one finds dogs that will never bite humans as well as others that will do serious protection work, not to mention all shades of gray in between.

Police-service dogs need to be focused on the adversary, not some piece of equipment the decoy may or may not be wearing. On the other hand, it is nice to be able to reward the dog with a sleeve drop on occasion. Fortunately, there are ways to do both, but to do so, the decoy and the handler must be coordinated. There are two major approaches, each working well on different dogs. The first is to work the dog on the stake line, dropping the sleeve at one end of a pass (see Figure 8.15). In this case, instead of leaving the area, you stop, wait a second, move laterally away from the sleeve, and then stimulate the dog again (see Figure 8.16). Many dogs will drop the sleeve immediately and move away from it to meet the new challenge (see Figure 8.17). Since you have no sleeve at this point, you know the dog is clearly showing aggression toward the man, not the sleeve.

Figure 8.15 The lateral sleeve drop: decoy and dog after the sleeve is dropped. (Photo by Darryl Lindsay)

Figure 8.16 The decoy leaving the dog and moving laterally. (Photo by Darryl Lindsay)

Figure 8.17 The dog leaving the sleeve and engaging the decoy. (Photo by Darryl Lindsay)

If it is necessary to test a sport-trained dog for police work, the above method is not a bad way to test for sleeve happiness. If the dog spits the sleeve out five times in a row to get at the returning decoy, she is probably a good candidate for police work. If she doesn't, perhaps she is not a good candidate. Some dogs have trouble with the above method, some because they are sleeve happy, others because they have a propensity for pain-induced and redirected aggression. As the decoy re-stimulates the latter type of dog, the dog redirects her aggression into the sleeve, which is close at hand, and simply bites the sleeve harder. The more you work a dog like that, the more she bites the sleeve. If you hit such a dog with a stick, again, she will just bite the sleeve harder, since any aggression that is stimulated gets redirected to the sleeve. It's a no-win situation. If you encounter this, another approach may work better.

When you drop the sleeve and freeze, the trainer will ask the handler to pick the dog up gently by the agitation collar or harness (not the choke collar) until the dog's front feet are just off the ground (see Figure 8.18). Wait patiently until the dog drops the sleeve. This may take a long while with some dogs, but most will

Figure 8.18 A dog thrashing the sleeve while the handler holds her front feet off the ground. (Photo by Darryl Lindsay)

eventually drop it. Choking the dog off does not teach what we wish the dog to learn, so the handler should avoid that if possible. When the dog releases the sleeve, move laterally and re-stimulate the dog. The handler should step laterally to follow you, carrying the dog away from the sleeve, which should be on the ground. When the dog is far enough away from the sleeve, the handler puts the dog's front feet back on the ground to let her respond to you, the decoy (see Figure 8.19). The handler should be careful during this exercise if the dog is prone to redirected aggression, since the handler is now the nearest available object.

If this method doesn't work well, take the dog off the stake line, have the handler hold the dog on leash, and try another variation, called the "linear sleeve drop." This time, when you drop the sleeve, the handler should pick the dog up by the collar as before (see Figure 8.20). When the dog releases the sleeve, the handler should step over it and walk forward several steps as you move away, stimulating the dog (see Figure 8.21). For some reason, it is easier for some dogs to make the switch this way.

Whatever way works, the point is to bring the dog back to the decoy when the sleeve is dropped. This teaches new dogs not to become sleeve happy even though the sleeve is dropped for

Figure 8.19 After the dog drops the sleeve, the handler moves laterally and places the dog back down in front of the decoy. The dog now engages the decoy. (Photo by Darryl Lindsay)

Figure 8.20 The linear sleeve drop. The handler holds the dog's front feet off the ground and waits for the dog to release the sleeve. (Photo by Laurie Mackenzie)

Figure 8.21 When the dog releases the sleeve, the handler steps forward over it and places the dog down in front of the decoy. (Photo by Laurie Mackenzie)

them sometimes, and it helps rehabilitate dogs who are already sleeve happy (although some of them never make a complete transition).

Hidden Sleeves

Another way to minimize problems with equipment orientation is to work the dog with hidden sleeves. This requires not only the sleeves but also many layers of loose clothing that can be thrown away when they are ripped. The main differences between this and external sleeve work is that it hurts the decoy more and bite placement is critical since your hand is often exposed. If you are a new decoy, the best way to try this method is to go back to the stake line with a good dog. Run your approaches the same way (see Figures 8.22 and 8.23), but make sure the bite is placed as near the elbow as possible (see Figure 8.24).

When the dog is on the sleeve, make sure you position your wrist higher than your elbow (see Figure 8.25). When dogs re-mouth or slip, gravity brings them down your arm. If the wrist is lower than the elbow, the dog will be slipping in the direction of the exposed hand. It is safer to keep the dog high on the forearm, as far away from the hand as possible. This is why you should pay strict attention to bite placement from the very first drills you

Figure 8.22 The author approaching a dog with the hidden sleeve on the side away from the dog. (Photo by Laurie Mackenzie)

Figure 8.23 Planting the foot to reverse direction and present the arm with the hidden sleeve. (Photo by Laurie Mackenzie)

Figure 8.24 Bite placement with the hidden sleeve. (Photo by Laurie Mackenzie)

Figure 8.25 After bite placement, the wrist should be held higher than the elbow. (Photo by Laurie Mackenzie)

run, even the ones with a human "dog" partner and the tape, as described previously. By the time you get to hidden sleeve work, your habits are formed and you will wish you had paid more attention to detail earlier in your training.

If you are working with unfamiliar dogs, it may be wise to wear a hand protector, although dogs can tell easily what they are. Also remember that most hidden sleeves have some bulk to them. Having one sleeve on and nothing on the other arm makes it easy for the dog to tell that you are wearing one (even humans can see the difference). Anything that shows you are protected in any way destroys the illusion you are trying to create for the dog: that you are unprotected. Consequently, it is best to wear the hidden sleeve on the arm farthest away from the dog. Focus the dog on the unprotected arm by making arm motions with it (see Figures 8.22 and 8.23). When turning toward the dog to change direction at the end of the pass, the protected arm can be slipped between your body and the dog. At the same time, move in close enough to allow the dog to make contact (see Figures 8.23 and 8.24). This gives the dog little time to notice the hidden sleeve.

Since the dog was focused on an unprotected arm, she makes the decision to bite an unprotected arm. By the time she notices the difference, the decision is past. Whether it is this deception or simply that most dogs decide that many humans wear hidden sleeves and it is all right to bite them, skillful use of hidden sleeves helps produce a good street dog.

Muzzles

Another useful tool in decoying is the muzzle. When a dog is wearing one, you can work her without wearing an external sleeve—although dogs can orient their behavior to the muzzle just as much as they do to external sleeves if the work is not balanced enough with a variety of exercises. But this is true of all equipment used during decoying.

The original purpose of working a dog in a muzzle was to allow the dog to strike the trunk of the body, thus focusing her away from the arms and legs. The dog learned that she could defeat a human even without biting (a big confidence builder); that hitting the trunk of the body can knock the human down; and that body slamming, punching with the paws, and tripping are effective tools. When done properly, muzzle work focuses a dog away from the hands and feet and onto the trunk of the body and teaches her to use all of her tools, making her a more complete fighter. Remember that anything you can do in a bite suit you can do with a muzzle, except test the bite, and there are some things you can do with a muzzle that cannot be done with a bite suit. One of the big advantages of muzzle work is that it allows you work the dog with no protective clothing at all. In fact, many dogs benefit from being rewarded for trying to bite a human wearing nothing but a bathing suit or shorts and T-shirt. This is particularly important in warm climates, where dogs quickly learn that only people with long sleeves can be hiding a hidden sleeve and therefore are the only ones worthy of attention. When you have nothing but a bathing suit on, the dog knows you aren't asking her to bite protective devices under the sleeves or trouser legs. It helps many dogs to stay focused on the human rather than arm or leg sleeves. Think about it: How can you teach a dog to bite people in shorts, T-shirts, or underwear if the decoys always wear bite suits and sleeves? Clearly, such bulky and easily visible equipment is not a good choice for this part of the service dog's training. To have a well-rounded dog, you need to do good muzzle work.

> **When done properly, muzzle work focuses a dog away from the hands and feet and onto the trunk of the body and teaches her to use all of her tools, making her a more complete fighter.**

In aggression control, the muzzle is often a benefit when teaching difficult dogs to release the decoy after biting. A general rule for the muzzle is that if the teeth are part of the problem, the muzzle may be part of the solution. If the dog continues her aggression after you cease displaying aggression-stimulating signals and the handler has given the release command, the handler can mold good behavior by physically helping the dog to assume the proper position and then emphatically rewarding the dog. This will teach the desired behavior without you having to resort to heavy-handed techniques. This allows us to reward good behavior instead of punishing bad behavior, which is always a good thing. The dog cannot resist our control by sinking her teeth into the decoy and hanging on for long periods if she cannot get her teeth into the decoy in the first place. The muzzle eliminates that complication completely, and if we reward the dog effectively for good behavior, she will not want to disobey. It's a very effective system for many dogs, so don't give up on control until you have tried the muzzle.

Agitation muzzles are different from regular muzzles, so be sure that the dog has one that allows her to breathe and bark but doesn't come off when put on properly. Also make sure that no teeth can stick through any openings, as stray teeth can inflict bad gashes (see Figures 8.26 and 8.27).

Figure 8.26 The agitation muzzle allows the dog to breathe and bark without restriction. (Photo by Laurie Mackenzie)

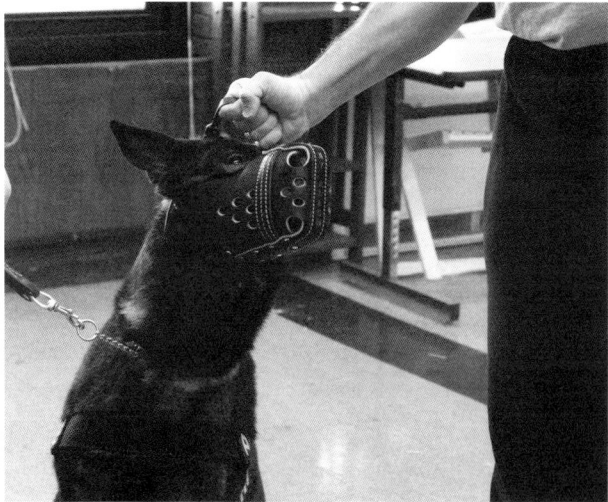

Figure 8.27 The decoy checking the fit of the muzzle. (Photo by Lauren Anderson)

Before using the muzzle in aggression work, the dog should have worn it frequently during obedience training, other assignments, and down time so that she adjusts to it, ignores it, and focuses through it mentally. Playing soccer or some ball game while muzzled often helps, or the handler could also let the muzzled dog bash her favorite toy around. If you put the muzzle on just during aggression, many dogs will spend their time trying to get it off instead of confronting the decoy. If the dog tries to claw it off when you appear, you know that the dog is not yet acclimated to the muzzle and is not ready for muzzle work. The handler should use it frequently during obedience training, and the dog should learn that she can never refuse her handler when he or she tells her the game is over and she must give up the ball or toy.

When to start muzzle work is a controversial topic. Some trainers feel that using the muzzle requires a dog with a high level of aggression. They say that if you put a dog into this type of work without sufficient aggression levels, it will be over-faced (confronted by something it can't handle) and psychological damage will be done that is often difficult to repair. They feel that muzzle work should be put off until the dog with medium aggression levels has had time to develop higher levels. However, other trainers have reported good success using muzzles even with weak dogs. Both sides agree that dogs with naturally high levels of aggression can begin muzzle work any time the trainer feels it is appropriate. If a trainer is unsure about whether or not to start this kind of work, it is probably safer to delay until he or she is sure.

As the decoy, you probably should not engage in muzzle work until your confidence in your work as a decoy is developed. Many people find muzzle work more disturbing emotionally than other forms of decoying. If you are one of them, do not get down on yourself for being a wimp. You will get used to it with time and positive exposure. The only question is how long it will take. Wearing a muzzle vest can help the new decoy since it is important for decoys to allow the dog to strike the trunk of the body and not protect themselves with their hands, which is the natural reaction of most people. The vest can be used for a while, but eventually you must abandon it, like all other protective equipment. At this point, you can minimize concussion by doing everything at close range, but remember that good muzzle work still inflicts a certain amount of pain on the decoy.

One popular method of introducing new decoys to muzzle work is to put the dog on the stake line again, at least for the first few sessions, so the decoy will feel comfortable. You should make sure you are wearing thick enough clothing to absorb the pressure of the dog's toenails, which can make nasty welts on human skin. If you are supposed to have minimal clothing on, insist that the dog wear boots over her toenails. You should also test each muzzle yourself by standing in front of the dog, grasping the muzzle by the sides with both hands, and pulling strongly toward you to see if you can pull the muzzle off the front of the dog's head (you should not twist or pinch the dog when doing this). The final test is to place a hand under the top strap of the muzzle with the palm of the hand facing up. Grasping the strap, twist your hand back toward you, trying to pry the muzzle off. Many times, a muzzle that will not come off any other way will come right off using this prying method. It has become the favorite method of muzzle testing for many decoys and handlers (see Figure 8.27).

When all is ready, you begin work normally. If the dog is confused, it may help if you put an external sleeve on for the first few sessions, until the dog realizes that she is supposed to show aggression. When the time is right for a bite, move close enough to allow the dog to make contact with your body, holding the arms up or back out of the way, falling to the ground the instant the dog strikes. Then, use distance-decreasing signals and crawl off as though injured (see Figures 8.28 and 8.29). As the dog becomes bolder, you can fall at the dog's feet and let her stand over you (the ultimate signal of dominance and victory for the dog) (see

Figure 8.28 The decoy allowing a muzzled dog to knock him down on first contact. (Photo by Laurie Mackenzie)

Figure 8.29 The decoy crawling away, using distance-decreasing signals. (Photo by Laurie Mackenzie)

Figure 8.30). As the dog's confidence rises, you can stand up for a few seconds before falling down, extending this time until it is not necessary to fall down for some time (see Figure 8.31).

It is important in all phases of muzzle work that you allow the dog to strike the trunk of your body without hindrance. This is difficult for some people, since the first instinct of a human being is to protect the body proper by catching incoming objects with the hands or to deflect things that might hurt the trunk of the body. The trick to muzzle work is to hold your hands and arms back,

Figure 8.30 The dog standing over the fallen decoy. (Photo by Laurie Mackenzie)

Figure 8.31 Eventually the dog will fight standing up. (Photo by Laurie Mackenzie)

exposing your body, and to take the hit in the ribs, back, or stomach without using your hands or arms to catch or cover up. This, of course, results in pain and bruising and is the reason muzzle vests were invented. New decoys will find protective vests an advantage at first, but, as I've already noted, eventually you have to eliminate them from your work and do "realistic" work with the muzzled dog.

Using your hands too much during this work can encourage some dogs to focus on them instead of your arms and body. Consequently, good decoys try to fight the dog using their forearms when doing muzzle work, keeping their hands back and out of the way. Keep your hands closed to prevent your fingertips from getting through the mesh of the muzzle and being bitten off by the dog. Good decoys are careful not to strike the dog with the elbows in the midst of the action.

The next step in this kind of work is to take the dog off the stake line, and you can work on moving bites in a similar manner to what you do in external sleeve work. When the short pursuits begin, it is often helpful if you fall down as soon as the dog makes contact (see Figure 8.32). It is important that you use your hands to cover your eyes and ears when this is happening (see Figure 8.33).

Figure 8.32 The decoy falling during an off-line muzzle pursuit. (Photo by Laurie Mackenzie)

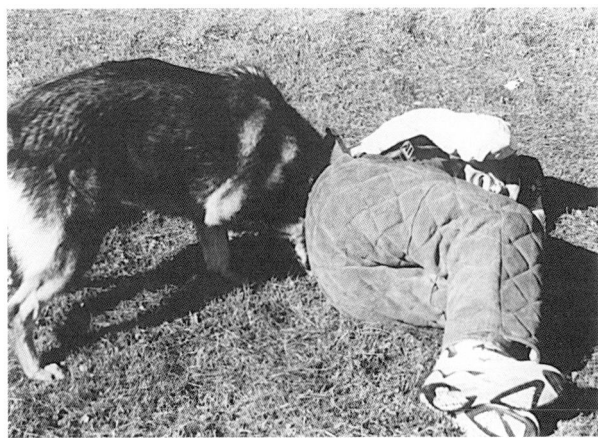

Figure 8.33 The decoy covering up while on the ground during muzzle pursuit. (Photo by Laurie Mackenzie)

The dog usually comes back and begins biting, or trying to bite, the prostrate, rolling, or crawling decoy. Even though her teeth are ineffective, it is simple for the dog to rip the decoy's ears and eyes with her toenails during this process. Remember that by lowering your height and using distance-decreasing signals, you stimulate predatory aggression. In this situation, many dogs will bite and claw at your head and neck more frequently than in other circumstances. This is natural, since the object of predatory aggression is to kill the prey animal to eat it. Neck and head bites do more efficiently lead to the death of the prey, so you should protect your head and neck as well as possible, even though you will probably get bashed by the muzzle on all parts of your body before you get up.

For next steps, as before, stay up for an instant before falling down, increasing the amount of time you stand erect according to the dog's confidence levels and willingness to fight (see Figures 8.34 and 8.35).

Once the dog is confident enough for you to remain standing, the trainer can conduct all the drills that can be done with a regular bite sleeve, including handler protection, control work, pursuits, and drills that include the termination of pursuit before the dog makes contact with the decoy.

Figure 8.34 The decoy beginning to stand. (Photo by Laurie Mackenzie)

Figure 8.35 The decoy standing. (Photo by Laurie Mackenzie)

Figure 8.36 Decoy Kyle McCraith running away from the dog and tapping his back to help focus the dog on his back. (Photo by Lauren Anderson)

Another useful sequence is to put the muzzled dog on a long line held by the handler after testing the fit of the muzzle, as in Figure 8.27. Work the dog normally, using the signals that stimulate the type of aggression desired by the trainer—social, defensive, or predatory. At the conclusion of this signaling, turn and run away, exposing your back and giving the dog a target by tapping your back with your hands (see Figure 8.36). When the dog makes physical contact of any kind on any part of your body, fall down, being careful not to fall on the dog. When you hit the ground, roll away from the dog and allow her to hit you repeatedly with the muzzle. Continue to brush the dog one way with your forearms and roll the other way to create a small amount of distance and to allow the dog to come back and hit you repeatedly until the trainer determines that the dog has done enough (see Figures 8.37, 8.38, 8.39, 8.40, 8.41, and 8.42). As mentioned previously, remember to

Figure 8.37 The dog rising to the target. (Photo by Lauren Anderson)

Figure 8.38 The dog hitting the decoy solidly in the back. (Photo by Lauren Anderson)

Figure 8.39 The decoy brushing the dog off after falling. Note the closed hands and use of only the forearms. (Photo by Lauren Anderson)

Figure 8.40 The decoy rolling away from the dog. (Photo by Lauren Anderson)

Figure 8.41 The decoy continuing to roll; the dog continuing to attack. Note the dog's intense focus on the decoy's shoulders and head. (Photo by Lauren Anderson)

Figure 8.42 Finally, the dog gets to stand over his vanquished foe. (Photo by Lauren Anderson)

keep your hands clenched to prevent your fingertips from getting through the mesh of the muzzle and being bitten. Also remember not to slap the dog but rather to brush her off, using your forearms, since the purpose of muzzle work is to focus the dog away from the hands and feet and onto the trunk of the body. The more you use your hands, the more you fight the reason for doing muzzle work in the first place. Many people have difficulty remembering this.

When the dog is strong and reliable at hitting your back, the trainer may increase the drill by having you turn to face the dog just before contact while still running backward away from her and patting your chest for a target (see Figures 8.43 and 8.44). This helps the dog learn to channel from purely predatory signals to a mixture of predatory and social signals on the way to handling the more challenging social signals all by themselves later. Again, when the dog makes contact, you should fall down and roll to finish the drill with ground fighting. Be aware that some dogs come up high enough to strike the chin or face at this stage.

When the dog is strong at hitting your chest, the trainer will increase the drill by having you stop running backward before

COMMON PROCEDURES

Figure 8.43 While running away, the decoy turns to face the dog, still moving backward away from her, tapping his chest to give the dog a target. (Photo by Lauren Anderson)

Figure 8.44 The dog moments after hitting the decoy in the chest, knocking him down. (Photo by Lauren Anderson)

contact and simply stand still to take the hit. At this point, something must be done to decrease the force of impact to protect both you and the dog. A common approach to this is for you to form a ramp with your body to deflect or ricochet the dog off of you when contact is made. This is illustrated in Figure 8.45, where you can see the decoy leaning back to form the ramp from the low point of the lead foot up through his shoulders. Wherever the dog makes contact, the force will be deflected up and to the side, lessening the impact on both dog and decoy. You can further help deflect the force by brushing the dog to the side with your forearms when the dog makes contact. As before, when the dog makes contact, fall to the ground and finish the drill with ground fighting (see Figures 8.46, 8.47, 8.48, and 8.49).

When the dog is strong at this phase of the drill, the trainer will ask you to remain on your feet after first contact. Deflect the dog and brush off her body, creating a small amount of distance

Figure 8.45 Decoy Kyle McCraith forming the ramp. (Photo by Lauren Anderson)

Figure 8.46 The force of impact being deflected up and to the side. (Photo by Lauren Anderson)

Figure 8.47 The decoy beginning to rotate and fall. (Photo by Lauren Anderson)

Figure 8.48 The decoy continuing to rotate before falling. (Photo by Lauren Anderson)

Figure 8.49 The decoy going down to begin ground fighting. (Photo by Lauren Anderson)

between the two of you, which you then increase by taking a few steps away from the dog and setting up in another ramped position for another hit (see Figures 8.50, 8.51, 8.52, 8.53, 8.54, and 8.55). When the dog makes contact a second time, fall to the ground and roll away from the dog to end the drill with ground fighting. It is important to set up for the second hit and stop moving your legs as quickly as possible, since leg movement focuses the dog's attention on the legs and the purpose of muzzle work is to focus the dog away from the legs and arms and onto the trunk of the body. As previously stated, many people have difficulty remembering this. When the dog is strong at the "two hits" part of this drill, the trainer will increase the drill to have you take three hits before falling. Eventually the dog will fight you for several minutes, knowing that if she just hits you enough times, you will eventually fall.

You can also use a muzzle to encourage the dog to bite specific parts of the body. Scenarios can be invented in which you flee and

Figure 8.50 The decoy taking the first hit. Note the ramped position and the wide arms that allow the dog full access to the trunk of his body. (Photo by Lauren Anderson)

Figure 8.51 The decoy beginning to brush the dog off while still standing. (Photo by Lauren Anderson)

Figure 8.52 Brush off continues—note that the decoy is not using his hands. (Photo by Lauren Anderson)

Figure 8.53 The dog falling back to the ground. (Photo by Lauren Anderson)

Figure 8.54 The decoy preparing to step back and form another ramp. (Photo by Lauren Anderson)

Figure 8.55 Moments after the second hit, before the decoy goes down to begin ground fighting. (Photo by Lauren Anderson)

leave only your legs hanging over the top of the fence, or through the gap you are stuck in, so that the dog must bite your legs or get nothing at all. Dogs that work with good decoys and muzzles can be taught any form of body bite desired.

REWARDS IN MUZZLE WORK

Before leaving the topic of muzzle work, it is worthwhile reviewing the topic of rewards. Many police-dog basic schools have trained dogs completely in muzzles until the last week when they test the dog's willingness to bite by putting the decoy in a bite suit. When properly worked and rewarded by the decoys, these dogs have no problem and perform as well as any others when deployed on the street. This would not be possible if the bite were the major reward for the dog. It is important for decoys to understand and accept that the bite is not the major reward in canine aggression. The bite is merely a tool that the dog uses to get the major reward. If the dog is exhibiting social aggression, she is working to see submission and respect in the adversary, and that is the major reward. It is the submission and respect that the dog wants, and if she has to bite to obtain this, she will. If submission can be achieved through some other behavioral tool (such as muzzle work), that is acceptable, too, and as long as the end result is obtained, the dog feels strongly rewarded. If the dog is exhibiting predatory aggression, she is seeking the capture and possible dispatching of the prey. If she has to chase and bite the prey to achieve this, she will. If the capture or dispatching can be achieved through some other activity (such as muzzle work), this is also acceptable, and as long as the method results in the capture of the prey, the dog feels strongly rewarded. If the dog is exhibiting defensive or fear-based aggression, she wants the frightening thing to become less scary. If she has to bite to make this happen, she will. If she can achieve this goal through some other behavior (such as muzzle work), this is acceptable, and as long as the scary thing becomes less scary, the dog feels strongly rewarded. As you can see, in all cases, you and your behavior are her major reward, not the bite. Service dogs in training can go long periods without actually biting anything and not suffer in performance if decoys are giving the proper rewards through their behaviors and actions.

> **In all cases of aggression training, it is the decoy and the decoy's behavior that are the major reward, not the bite. Service dogs in training can go long periods without actually biting anything and not suffer in performance if decoys are giving the proper rewards through their behaviors and actions.**

Bite or Body Suits

Another useful tool for the decoy is the bite suit. It allows you to focus the dog on any part of the body except your head. While it is an extremely useful tool, remember that it is only one in a collection of tools, all of which should be used to create a balanced service dog. People are prone to fads, where one tool becomes more popular than the others and gets used too much at the expense of the others. At the time of this writing, the fad is the bite suit. While it is a valuable part of a dog's development, some trainers are working their dogs on nothing else but bite suits and others are overemphasizing it horribly. Police dogs should be comfortable biting anything and should be worked on all types of equipment frequently so that they are accustomed to variety. This way, when they meet strange and unpredictable things on the street, they are more comfortable dealing with changes and weirdness, and they tend to perform better. This variety cannot be achieved when the decoy works only or mostly in a bite suit. The ability to handle variety and strangeness is the name of the game for dogs that must work in the real world, so we must balance their exposure to different types of equipment appropriately.

Working in a bite suit is similar to using other equipment and going through the procedures described above in that it requires the same approach angles, timing, and balance, among other skills and techniques. Working in a bite suit does require you to practice more in the beginning to master the mechanics of balance and movement (which are more difficult in a suit). Once the suit is mastered, you can focus the dog on different body parts by moving them more and making them more interesting than the other parts of the body, or arranging the situation so that the only place the dog can bite is the body part you want her to bite. Decoys are often safer in suits than outside them, which is important when you are working with unknown or unstable dogs. Suits can offer big advantages in many situations.

One popular method for introducing dogs to the bite suit is to again put the dog on a stake line or back tie so you can better judge distances and angles. Work the dog normally, stimulating whatever type of aggression the trainer desires, but when you move in to offer the dog a bite, raise your arm differently. Instead of bringing your arm up in front of your body to present it like you do with an external or hidden sleeve, pull your arm back and raise it out of reach of the dog, presenting your body and back instead of your arm (see Figures 8.56 and 8.57). The dog can be worked to re-grip if necessary,

Figure 8.56 Decoy Joe Lutkowski (a.k.a. "Pocono Joe") raising his arm before crossing in front of the dog to present his side and back. (Photo by Matt Nero)

Figure 8.57 The decoy presenting his side and back instead of his arm. (Photo by Matt Nero)

the top of the suit can be stripped off or dropped when needed, or you can carefully go prone to reward the dog for good work. When prone, it is useful to have the leg of a standing person to hold onto so the dog cannot drag you into an unsafe area.

To encourage the dog to target your back from a distance, you can begin working by back-peddling away from the dog, focusing her on one of your hands (see Figure 8.58). Continue to do this as

Figure 8.58 The great Franco Angelini at work focusing the dog on his hand. (Photo by John Johnston)

the dog is released, but raise your arm and pivot with your feet just before contact, so the arm and hand the dog has been focusing on cannot be reached, making your back the only available target (see Figures 8.59, 8.60, and 8.61).

You can also focus the dog on the front of your body by tucking your arm back and moving only your shoulder and chest while facing the dog, thereby encouraging her to bite either your chest or inner arm. If the bite is particularly solid, the dog's body can even be shifted up onto your opposite shoulder and lowered back down to end the drill, with you (carefully) descending to the ground to reward the dog (see Figures 8.62, 8.63, 8.64, and 8.65).

Figure 8.59 The decoy beginning to pivot. (Photo by John Johnston)

Figure 8.60 The decoy taking his arm away, leaving his back as the only good target. (Photo by John Johnston)

Figure 8.61 The dog properly placed on the decoy's back. (Photo by John Johnston)

COMMON PROCEDURES

Figure 8.62 Franco Angelini focusing the dog for a frontal bite. (Photo by John Johnston)

Figure 8.63 The dog taking a solid bite. (Photo by John Johnston)

Figure 8.64 When a good bite is solid, nothing disturbs it. (Photo by John Johnston)

Figure 8.65 The decoy ending the drill by going down carefully to reward the dog. The dog learns that if she takes a solid bite and holds on through everything, she can always take down the giant. (Photo by John Johnston)

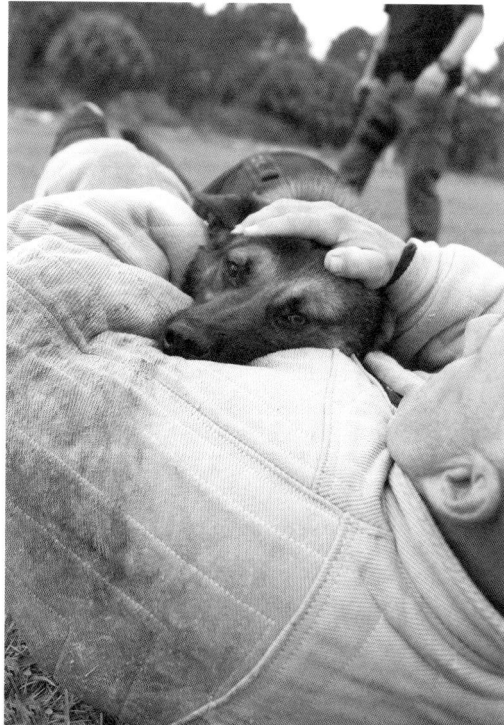

Stick Work

Stick work can be introduced during any of the above phases of decoying, although many decoys are highly distracted when they first start hidden-sleeve or muzzle work (they are worried about their physical safety). And when they first start wearing a bite suit, they can hardly move. So, most do better if sticks and weapons are introduced after they are confident in their ability to move in a bite suit, can take real bites, and survive muzzle work. While it may be done at any time, it might be wise to first work with sticks with dogs on the stake line, and after you are somewhat experienced. As you did in the drills without dogs, you can begin by using the stick on the stake line itself just behind the dog's collar, first just stroking the line gently, then progressing to light taps, and finally to stinging blows, but all on the line itself. When you have mastered that, you can work off the stake line, controlling the stick on the dog herself after she makes contact with the sleeve. Try to remember to use the stick only when you are moving toward the sleeve or when you are giving distance-increasing (or challenging) signals, as is explained in chapter 7.

Blank Cartridges

While we are talking about weapons, a word or two about blank guns is probably in order. It seems that dogs can tell the difference in frequencies between different calibers. It is possible to have a dog that is confident when a .38 caliber blank is fired and yet gun shy when a .25 caliber blank is fired. Fortunately, this is not common, but it happens enough to make it advisable to work your dogs on different calibers.

Blank guns are not as safe as everyone thinks, either. While it is true no projectile comes out of the barrel, it is not true that *nothing* comes out of the barrel. Most large-caliber blank cartridges have a wad to hold the powder in. These wads are shot out of an unblocked barrel when the gun discharges and are quite capable of inflicting damage. They can strike people in the face, causing damage, including blindness. Dogs are not immune to this type of injury. They can also break windows and knock objects off desks and shelves. If you are dealing with shotguns, the wads are large enough to do serious damage in several ways. It is best to treat blank guns very carefully. They should not be aimed into the face of any animal (humans included) at close range and probably should not be aimed directly at any part of a human body when it is not an absolute necessity.

Even more dangerous is the practice of using blanks in real service weapons. This is good for realism, and actually required by some certification standards, but use extreme caution. Live ammunition at the wrong time would be deadly. Any good firearms instructor can tell you that human beings make mistakes. Documented stories abound regarding officers who had accidental discharges with weapons they thought were empty; or who rushed into dangerous situations with empty sidearms (they forgot to reload); or who died trying to fire a semiautomatic with the safety still engaged; or who went on duty forgetting to replace the blanks used in training with live rounds. It is unreasonable to assume that you will not make a mistake. Everyone makes them.

The trick is to develop habits that ensure the gun is in a safe condition when you make your mistake. So, if you cannot obtain or make weapons with blocked barrels (the best alternative) at least have a rule that two separate people check the condition of every service weapon and its ammunition before it is used. Also avoid aiming it directly at dogs or humans. "Someday," when you make your mistake, you will be glad you have those safety measures in place. Probability says that someday someone is going to shoot someone accidentally. Make sure that it is someone else, not you. Remember that two separate people should also check every service weapon and its ammunition before it is returned to duty.

Whips

There has been a lot of interest in whips lately. They can be used in many different ways, but the best is for auditory stimulation. The sound of a whip has a definite effect on some dogs, stimulating them to higher levels of aggression. Sled-dog drivers have used this effect during races for a long time, and now decoys are benefiting from it. Actually, we have been using auditory stimulation for years. Many old-time trainers still like to fire blank guns during decoy work, feeling that it makes the dogs more aggressive. This is true, but it was the source of many tactical problems until we learned to train dogs for a neutral reaction to gunfire. Just as a dog reacts to a blank, so she will react to the sound of a whip cracking. Naturally, this means you can create the problem of having dogs show aggression every time they hear something that sounds like a whip if you don't balance its use properly. A whip can be used to inflict pain on a dog, but that is not its best use. Small amounts of pain are best applied with other items, and hitting dogs with whips is a public-relations disaster looking for a place to happen. Be careful. Better yet, be wise.

If you master the common procedures and tools described in this chapter, you should be able to adjust to other procedures as trainers work with you. You won't hurt dogs by making basic mistakes, and you should be useful in the production of police-service dogs as you gain experience. If you can work your way through this book under the tutelage of a good trainer and decoy, you will have a good start in one of the most fascinating phases of police-dog training. Good luck.

Notes

Chapter 2

1. American College of Sports Medicine, *ACSM Fitness Book* (Champaign, IL: Leisure Press, 2003).

Chapter 5

1. William T. James in Charles R. Stockard, *The Genetic and Endocrinic Basis for Differences in Form and Behavior* (Philadelphia: The Wistar Institute of Anatomy and Biology, 1941). See also John Paul Scott and John L. Fuller, *Dog Behavior: The Genetic Basis* (Chicago: University of Chicago Press, 1965).
2. Examples are described by Katherine Houpt and Malcolm Willis, "Genetics of Behavior," in A. Ruvinsky and J. Sampson, eds., *The Genetics of the Dog* (New York: CABI Publishing, 2001).
3. See Carmelo Battaglia, *Breeding Better Dogs* (Atlanta, GA: BEI, 1984). Discussions of the interactions of genetics, development, and adult learning on dog behavior can also be found in Frederick J. Sautter and John A. Glover, *Behavior, Development and Training of the Dog* (New York: ARCO Publishing Company, Inc., 1978).
4. This topic is reviewed by K.E. Moyer, "Kinds of Aggression and Their Physiological Basis," *Communications in Behavioral Biology* 2, no. A (1968): 65–87.
5. Figure 5.1 is adapted from M. Fox, *Understanding Your Dog* (New York: Coward, McCann and Goeghegan, 1972).

Index

A
adult learning, 45–47, 52–53
aggression, as a behavior
  affective forms, 54–55
  non-affective forms, 55–56
  factors affecting aggression, 45–53
aggression, stimulation of, 70–77
aggression, types of
  fear-induced, 55
  idiopathic, 56, 67
  inter-male, 55, 61
  irritable, 56, 65
  learned, 55, 64
  maternal, 55, 63–64
  pain-induced, 55, 57–60
  play, 56, 66–67
  predatory, 56, 65–66
  protective, 55, 63
  redirected, 55, 64–65
  sexual, 56, 65
  social, 55
  territorial, 55–57
agitator, 1
amygdala, 54
androgens, 55

B
back tie, 84–85
bark, 10–11
behavior inhibition system, 52
Bekoff's play bow, 21–22, 67
bites
  full mouth, 15
  typewriter, 15
  not the reward for aggression, 70, 140–141
body axis, 18
body language, 15

C
canine communication
  auditory, 9–12
  olfactory, 12
  tactile, 13–15
  visual, 15–32
catcher, 1
channeling the dog, 78
chemistry, 48–50
cocking the dog, 108
concussion, 97

D
decoy, 1
decoy as a tool, 2
decoy's purpose, 1–4
distance decreasing signals, 31–32, 69
distance increasing signals, 30–31, 69
Dog Appeasing Pheromone (DAP), 48

INDEX

drills without dogs, 87–100
drives, 43–45
dropping the sleeve, 111–116

E
early experience, 50–52
energy level, 17
escape reaction, 60

F
fear scent, 12
fitness, 6–7
flanking, 34, 57–59
footwear, 86

G
genetics, 45–48, 53
growl, 9

H
hackles, 23
head, 24
helper, 1
high energy, 17
hormones, 49
howl, 11–12
hypothalamus, 54

I
imprint process, 52, 53
inverted "U", 80–81

L
lateral hypothalamus, 54
long mouth, 26
low energy, 17

M
mesolimbic reward pathway, 45, 52
motivation, 43–45
moving the dog, 99
muscle tone, 2
muzzle work, 120–141

N
neck, 23
neonatal period, 50
neophobia, 61
neutralizing the dog, 108
neurotransmitters
   acetylcholine, 52
   dopamine, 45, 52
   serotonin, 48

O
observational learning, 51
one time "No!", 13–14

P
paw lifting, 22
physical requirements, 5–7
primary fear period, 52
progestins, 49
pseudo-pregnant aggression, 64
punishment, 13–14
punishment circuit, 52

Q
quarry, 2

R
reading the dog, 16
retirement, 7
rewarding aggression, 70–77, 140–141
rewards in muzzle work, 140–141

S
sack work, 102–107
scratch pants, 86–87
sensitive periods of development, 50
short mouth, 26
showing eye, 24
signals
   arousal, 30
   distance decreasing, 31–32, 69
   distance increasing, 30–31, 69
sleeves
   external, 107–116
   hidden, 116–120

sleeve-happy dogs, 111
slinking, 20
slipping the sleeve, 111–116
socialization period, 50–52
stake line, 84–85
standing over another dog, 21
state of arousal, 17
stimulating aggression, 70–77
stride, 20

T
tail, 27
tapetum, 24
testosterone, 49
T-ing up, 19

transition period, 50
tug work, 102–107

V
ventromedial hypothalamus, 54
voice tone or pitch, 9–11

W
wedge, 107
whine, 9

Y
yelp, 9
Yerkes-Dodson Law, 80–81

Author Biography

Dr. Stephen A. "Doc" Mackenzie (1948–2021) held a PhD in the genetics of behavior from Cornell University and was a professor at the State University of New York at Cobleskill for almost 40 years, where he taught genetics, canine training, care and training of the working dog, and canine management. In 2020, the university awarded him a Distinguished Service Professorship Award in recognition of his years of service, including his lead role in establishing the first canine training and management bachelor degree program in the United States.

Doc had been a deputy sheriff for the Schoharie County Sheriff's Office for 25 years, serving as their K9 handler and trainer for seven. He was rated a master trainer of utility, cadaver, narcotics, and wildlife detection dogs by the North American Police Work Dog Association (NAPWDA) and had been an executive board member of North East Wilderness Search and Rescue, Inc. and the president of the New York State Canine Association. Doc was also a nose work trial judge for the National Association of Canine Scent Work (NACSW), a court-recognized expert in animal behavior at state and federal levels in both criminal and civil cases, and a frequent instructor at police-dog seminars across the United States and Canada.

His other books include *Aggression Control: Teaching the "Out"* and *Police Officer's Guide to K9 Searches*, both published by Dog Training Press (dogtrainingpress.com).

K9 Professional Training Series

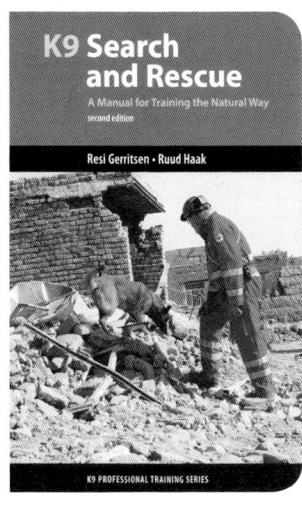

See the complete list at
dogtrainingpress.com